T0166865

AC/DC
IN THE STUDIO

JAKE BROWN

JOHN BLAKE

Published by John Blake Publishing Ltd,
3 Bramber Court, 2 Bramber Road,
London W14 9PB, England

www.johnblakepublishing.co.uk

www.facebook.com/Johnblakepub facebook
twitter.com/johnblakepub twitter

First published in hardback in 2010
This edition published in 2013

ISBN: 978 1 78219 426 2

British Library Cataloguing-in-Publication Data:

A catalogue record for this book is available from the British Library.

Design by www.envydesign.co.uk

Printed and bound in Great Britain by CPI Group (UK) Ltd

1 3 5 7 9 10 8 6 4 2

Papers used by John Blake Publishing are natural, recyclable products made from
wood grown in sustainable forests. The manufacturing processes conform to the
environmental regulations of the country of origin.

Every attempt has been made to contact the relevant copyright-holders,
but some were unobtainable. We would be grateful if the appropriate people
could contact us.

This book is dedicated to my lady Tina von Hagel, thank you for your light, you inspire me every day.

And to my godson Jackson Rollin Schuchard for kicking as much ass as this band does! You're a cool little dude, and I can't wait to take you, your pop and me to our first AC/DC concert together!

ABOUT THE AUTHOR

Nashville-based music biographer Jake Brown has published 25 books, including *Jane's Addiction: In the Studio*, Tracii Guns' forthcoming authorised memoir, *Heart: in the Studio* (co-written with Ann and Nancy Wilson), *Tupac: In the Studio* (authorised by the estate), as well as titles on Kanye West, R Kelly, Jay-Z, the Black Eyed Peas and non-hip hop titles including *Mötorhead: In the Studio* (co-written with Lemmy Kilmister). Brown is also a featured author in Rick James' autobiography, *Memoirs of Rick James: Confessions of a Super Freak* and is the co-author of *What the Hell Was I Thinking?!* by Jasmin St Claire. Brown was recently nominated alongside Lemmy Kilmister for the 2010 Association for Recorded Sound Collections Awards in the category of Excellence in Historical Recorded Sound Research. Brown is also owner of the hard rock label Versailles Records, distributed nationally by Big Daddy Music/MVD Distribution and celebrating its tenth anniversary in business this year.

ACKNOWLEDGEMENTS

This marks my 25th published book as a music biographer and I couldn't have picked a cooler band as the subject of my latest *In the Studio* book. Thanks for 35 years of fantastic rock 'n' roll!

Project thank you(s): first and foremost, AC/DC for continuing to give us the gift of your music – your rock 'n' roll resilience is our own as fans; to John Blake Publishing for releasing this especially personal book; to Mike Fraser, Tony Platt, Mark Opitz and Mark Dearnley for your amazing interviews; and to anyone/everyone else who contributed in one way or another to this project.

Reference notes: In addition to the countless referenced news publications used as sources in the course of researching and writing this book, I would also like to acknowledge music journalists including Murray Engleheart and Arnaud Durieux (*AC/DC: Maximum Rock & Roll*); Susan Masino (*Let There Be Rock: The Story of AC/DC*); Paul Stenning (*Two Sides to Every Glory: AC/DC – The Complete Biography*); Ethan Schlesinger and Heather Mills.

Personal thank you(s): First and foremost, I would like to thank James and Christina-Thieme Brown for continuing to tirelessly support my various artistic goings-on (both literary and musically); my brother Joshua T Brown (K-9 Catalyst, proud of you, bud); the extended Brown and Thieme Families; Alex Schuchard, thanks for consistently being my

ACKNOWLEDGEMENTS

surrogate sibling, best friend and now band-mate; Jackson Schuchard for being the coolest godson in the world!; Andrew and Sarah McDermott; 'The' Sean and Amy Fillinich; Adam Perri; Chris 'SEE' Ellauri; Matt, Eileen and Kamelya Ellen Peitz; Richard (thanks for the past ten years re Versailles), Lisa and Regan Kendrick; Paul and Helen Watts!; Bob O'Brien and Cayenne Engel; Lexi 'Clown' Federov; Rose Reiter and Gerry Plant; MVD Distribution/Big Daddy Music; Aaron 'Whippit' Harmon for continuing to have my back musically week in and out; Joe Viers/Sonic Lounge Studios for ten years of great ears; Andrew Neice @ Melodic Rock; Keavin Wiggins @ Antimusic.com; Cheryl Hoahing @ *Metal Edge*; Tim @ *BraveWords/Bloody Knuckles*; Rock and Roll Report; John Lavallo and Take Out Marketing; Larry, Joel, James, and everyone at Arbor Books.

To Jasmin St. Claire, thanks for hanging in there, we finally made it!; Lemmy Kilmister; Curt and Cris Kirkwood/Dennis; Ben Ohmart/BearManor Media; Jack, Crissy, David, Simon et al at ECW Press; Tony (get well soon) & Yvonne Rose at Amber Books; Aaron, Gabriel, Victor, John and everyone at SCB Distribution/Rock N Roll Books; Bookmasters; Jason Rothberg and Tracii Guns, thanks for the opportunity to be involved with telling this amazing story, 2011!!!; and finally and without arrogance of any sort implied, thank you to the music fans who buy and read my books, and specifically this series, as you keep them coming!

CONTENTS

INTRODUCTION

AC/DC IN THE STUDIO

AC/DC has reigned over rock 'n' roll for 35 years. Their signature power-chord rock has become the standard bearer of the sonic genre they helped to invent, while *Rolling Stone* has declared that they are 'one of the top hard-rock bands in history'. In a further testament to just how devout a fan base has followed the band from their Sydney, Australia roots around the globe time and again, the same magazine recently reported that 'the group has remained a major concert draw, and its albums consistently go platinum – despite never having had a Top 20 single in the US, [making them] one of the most enduringly popular hard-rock bands on the planet'. In spite of the band's lack of singles-chart history, their live set list reads like a three-volume Greatest Hits collection, from 'It's a Long Way to the Top (If You Wanna Rock 'n' Roll)' all the way to their seminal hits 'Highway to

Hell' and 'You Shook Me All Night Long'. Indeed, the band has written the soundtrack of a generation, with *Billboard* magazine declaring the latter song 'the greatest one-night-stand anthem in rock history'.

Having spawned what the magazine called 'countless imitators' over the next two decades, AC/DC's influence is felt today as much as ever, as evinced by the smash success of their October 2008 album *Black Ice*, which sold an astonishing 1,762,000 in its first week of release, making history by debuting at No. 1 on album charts in 29 countries simultaneously. The record would go on to sell seven million copies worldwide, spending several weeks on the top of the Billboard Top 200 Album Chart. The BBC would salute the band's longevity, highlighting the fact that 'way back in the late '70s the Aussie legends defined an almost platonic form of rock 'n' boogie that was hand built to last. Time has not withered them.' The band would vindicate this judgement in 2009 when they were honoured with the Best Hard Rock Performance Grammy, triumphing over Alice in Chains, Linkin Park, Nickelback and Metallica.

And so, as the band rocks on with a whole new generation of fans, we look back at the creation of a timelessly seminal catalogue of albums...

CHAPTER ONE

BAND DOWN UNDER

From 1975 to 1977, AC/DC was the hardest-working band in rock 'n' roll, releasing four studio albums in two years: *High Voltage* (1975), *T.N.T.* (1975), *Dirty Deeds Done Dirt Cheap* (1976) and *Let There Be Rock* (1977).

All four were recorded at Albert Studios in Sydney, Australia and produced by former Easybeats members Harry Vanda and George Young. According to their official website, this writing and production partnership 'created one of the great rock 'n' roll bands of the 1960s – The Easybeats – and wrote a string of classic hits that have stood the test of time... The Easys stormed to No. 1 in Australia in May 1965 and the ferocious phenomenon of "Easyfever" spiralled... With their vital, urgent sound the Easybeats gave Australian music a new identity and confidence. The hits came in ceaseless cascade

1

and overnight Australian pop and rock shifted from derivation and imitation to innovation.

'The song that still stands as the team's most admired, acclaimed and recorded piece, the working-class anthem, "Friday on my Mind" – a global hit for them – gave them the clout to begin writing and recording songs of sometimes extraordinary grandeur... Returning to Australia they put to use all they had learned... In a new state-of-the-art recording studio in King Street, Sydney they began a blitzkrieg of Australian popular music in a manner that has not been experienced since.'

As Angus Young, who grew up in the shadow of his older brother George's success, recalled in an interview with *Guitar Player* magazine, the Easybeats were 'definitely an inspiration. There was a hell of a lot that came from that band; they were the forerunners of a lot of things. They were at the time of the early stages, when people didn't know how to react.'

Brother Malcolm Young told *Mojo* magazine that 'all the males in our family played. Stevie, the oldest, played accordion. Alex and John were the first couple to play guitar, and being older it was sort of passed down to George, then myself, then Angus – like when you're kids and you get all your brothers' and sisters' hand-me-downs. We never realised that we were learning guitars – they were always just there. We thought that everyone was like that. Me and Angus

2

would just fiddle – 12-bars mainly, Chuck Berry, Little Richard, Elvis.'

Elaborating on some of their musical influences as they began to develop as guitar players, Angus recalled in an interview with *Guitar World* magazine that 'my sister took me to see Louis Armstrong when I was a kid, and I still think he was one of the greatest musicians of all time. Especially when you listen to his old records, like "Basin Street Blues" and "St James Infirmary", and hear the incredible musicianship and emotion coming out of his horn. And the technology in those days was almost nonexistent – all the tracks had to be done in one take. I can picture him in that big football stadium where I saw him. He wasn't a big man, but when he played, he seemed bigger than the stadium itself!'

The blues was also a major influence. Angus told rock journalist Heather Mills that, growing up, he listened to 'a lot of the Chicago thing and a lot of different players. Elmore James. I very much like his style of playing… And BB King is another one. Buddy Guy is a great player. And I like Johnny Winter. He's got a lot of power in his blues. For rock 'n' roll I like Chuck Berry's playing. His things are a bit of an art.'

For Angus, growing into his own style as a lead player was a natural evolution, as brother Malcolm told *Mojo*. 'Angus was the player, to be honest; he was always the showman of the two of us when we were kids.' As for his own influences, Malcolm recalled in an interview with *Guitar Player*, 'I got my ear into Eric Clapton with John Mayall's *Blues Breakers*, as well as the Paul Butterfield Blues Band, and things like that. George was in London and I used to ask him, "Pick me out anything that you think is good at the moment," and he'd send me over a parcel of albums. He was a good help to us.'

In spite of their development as players, Angus revealed in the same interview, 'Mal and me were kept away from [guitars]. In school, you got frowned upon because obviously your brother and your family was an influence to rebel. At that time, it was better for us not to be sort of pushed at it. My parents thought we'd be better off doing something else.'

But, despite his parents' efforts, Malcolm recalled with a smile that they couldn't keep the family free of the rock 'n' roll mania that followed the Easybeats everywhere. 'We were getting all these screaming girls, a couple of hundred of them, hanging outside our house for a glimpse of the Easybeats, who were like Australia's Beatles… Those were great days. I was just going into puberty… [and] me and Angus used to hang out there with them thinking, "This is the way to go!" That planted the seed for us and made us play more, try harder.'

While big brother George was definitely an influence on Angus, it was actually rhythm guitarist/songwriter Malcolm who first recruited Angus into AC/DC. 'Malcolm was putting together a band,' Angus recalled. 'He found a condemned building in Newtown and said he could get it for a couple of bucks. He was just auditioning guys and telling people to come down and try out. A week later he said to me, "Why don't you bring your guitar down and try out?" I thought, "Great – anything but a day job."'

After working through several singers (including original singer Dave Evans), they encountered Ronald Belford 'Bon' Scott, who had also previously sung for The Valentines and Fraternity. Strangely, it wasn't a musical context that provided Angus with his first impression of Bon, but a talk show on Australian television. 'Something to do with some pop bloke nicking one of his songs and the interviewer was being totally condescending thinking he was this stupid rock 'n' roller,' Angus told *Mojo*. 'All of a sudden Bon was yelling, "Fucking cunt!" and leapt across the studio, diving on top of the pop bloke. I thought, "Hmm, pretty lively."'

Recalling his first actual meeting with the singer in September 1974, Angus told rock journalist Paul Stenning that, when 'Bon first came along and saw me and Malcolm, he sat behind the drums and started bashing away. We said, "We know a good rock 'n' roll drummer – what we want is a great rock 'n' roll singer," hence the song we recorded. This is what we wanted. For us, it was great – he was a striking person, he did have the stuff legends are based on.'

For the band's first gig with Bon, for example, Angus recounted to Masino, 'the only rehearsal we had was sitting around for an hour before the gig, pulling out every rock 'n' roll song we knew. When we finally got there, Bon downed about two bottles of Bourbon with dope, coke, speed and he says, "Right, I'm ready" – and he was too. He was fighting fit. There was this immediate transformation and he was running around yelling at the audience. It was a magic moment.'

Offering his own assessment of why Bon fitted so perfectly into the band's musical fold, drummer Phil Rudd told *Modern Drummer* magazine that the singer knew 'you don't come across guys like Malcolm and Angus very often... Bon wanted to be the drummer, but he was too good a singer.'

As for what the singer brought to the table in rounding out AC/DC's official line-up, Malcolm told Masino, 'Bon was the biggest single influence on the band. When he came in it pulled us together. He had that real "stick-it-to-em" attitude. We all had it in us, but it took Bon to bring it out.'

Angus took that assessment even further, saying to Miller, 'I don't think there would have been an AC/DC if it hadn't been for Bon. You might have got me and Malcolm doing something, but it wouldn't have been what it was. Bon moulded the character and flavour of AC/DC.'

Equally, Bon felt that AC/DC allowed him to discover his true soul and spirit as a lead vocalist. 'In the early days when I sang,' he explained to a British music journalist, 'I always felt that there was a certain amount of urgency to what I was doing. There was no vocal training in my background, just a lot of good whisky … I went through a period where I copied a lot of guys and found when I was singing that I was starting to sound just like them. But when I met up with [AC/DC], they told me to sound like myself, and I really had a free hand doing what I always wanted to do.'

With singer and band instantly kindred spirits on both musical and personal levels, Angus told Stenning that 'we saw more of Bon than his family did, especially us three. It was always me, Bon and Malcolm.'

So excited about the new sound they had discovered together, the band quickly set their sights on the recording studio, which for the newly installed singer turned out to be a doubly thrilling experience. 'Bon's biggest idol was actually George, going back to when he was in the Easybeats,' Angus told Masino. 'And when he came to see us for the first time, he said, "Well, I get to work with these two guys, and I get to work with their brother!"'

In an interview with *Brave Words / Bloody Knuckles* magazine years later, Malcolm explained that– even more than their excitement about the album – the band took most satisfaction in the fact that the dream they shared with thousands of other aspiring musicians was actually coming true: they didn't have to work for 'the man' any longer. Reflecting on their starting days, he recalled 'working our butts off, getting covered in oil and all the shit that goes with it, and when we got to play club gigs, luckily enough, we thought, "This is it! Don't have to work! Angus, we can make 50 bucks a week each here. We can survive without a day job." That was our big plan. So everything outside of a club gig is a bonus to us. We made it 25 years ago, as far as we're concerned!'

CHAPTER TWO

HIGH VOLTAGE (1975)/ T.N.T. (1975)/ DIRTY DEEDS DONE DIRT CHEAP (1976)

**'From the beginning people dismissed
us as a bar band'**
ANGUS YOUNG

So inspired were they by their new musical union that, as Malcolm Young told *Mojo*, 'within three weeks of Bon being in the band we had written all this new material and we were ready to record the first album'.

Quickly signed by brother George and his writing/ production partner Harry Vanda, AC/DC entered the studio in November, insulating themselves from day one from outside influences. Having dealt with the corporate record industry machine for years as a member of the Easybeats, George Young seemed to relish the freedom he and the band had from any corporate pressures as they set about crafting the band's debut LP. 'It was great to turn around and say, "Excuse me, I'm just gonna play a bit of rock music here,"' he recalled to journalist Martin Aston, 'and it was the best thing we've recorded for a while ... We just ignored the influence of the record company and any producers.'

Shortly afterwards, the band signed with Albert Records, a sister company to Albert Studios. According to the band's number-one fansite, crabsodyinblue.com, the company was founded by Jacques Albert, and to this day it stands as the oldest independent publishing house in Australia. 'Jacques Albert migrated to Australia from Switzerland in 1884 and set up as a music publisher. Jacques' son Sir Alexis Albert carried on the business and it would be one of his three sons that would help shape the fortunes of the Easybeats and AC/DC. Ted Albert, the middle son of three, helped form the offshoot record company Albert Productions. Ted set about signing the musical talent of Australia in the early 1960s. It was through a friend called Mike Vaughan that Ted first met an up-and-coming band by the name of the Easybeats. First impressions of the Easybeats stirred Ted and he promptly snapped the band up on a contract and Easyfever was born.

'After the short-lived success of the Easybeats on the international scene Ted Albert lured the mainstays of the band, George Young and Harry Vanda, back to Australia in 1973. The artist, however, that would consolidate the rebirth of Albert Productions as a force in the Australian record company industry would prove to be the signing of John Paul

Young (no relation). John Paul Young had a minor hit with the Vanda/Young composed track "Pasadena" in April 1972. It was this success that enabled Ted Albert to persuade George Young and Harry Vanda to run a recording studio for Albert Records. John Paul Young would later go on to be more remembered for the hit single "Love is in the Air".'

'Harry Vanda and George Young would go on to produce records for numerous Australian acts as well as working on various side projects themselves. It would be through Vanda and Young that Angus and Malcolm Young would have their first taste of the recording industry while working on the Marcus Hook Roll Band [a Vanda-Young studio project]. This early experience would prove valuable when AC/DC went on to record the early albums and singles for the Albert label under the guidance of George Young and Harry Vanda.'

The band set up shop with brother George and his partner Harry Vanda in the famed Studio 1 at Albert Productions, which *Studio Connections* magazine described as being 'one of the major recording studios in Australia from 1973 through to 1986. Originally known as Studio 139, Studio 1 was *the* rock 'n' roll recording studio in Sydney, with the likes of AC/DC, The Angels, Rose Tattoo, John Paul Young and many other famous Alberts artists recording there. As time went by and Alberts built more studios, this studio became used almost exclusively for in-house work only. It was the home of Vanda and Young…

'The walls and ceiling of the control room were black. The recording area was a large relatively live room with moveable curtains. Mirror tiles on the walls near the drum area made for a bright drum sound. One wall of this room was covered in the graffiti of many famous artists who recorded there. A second smaller room housed a Yamaha grand piano.'

When it came to deciding which songs passed muster for recording, Angus explained to rock journalist Susan Masino that George would take 'our meanest song and try it out on keyboards with arrangements like 10cc or Mantovani. If it was passed, the structure was proven, then we took it away and dirtied it up.'

Where attention turned to crafting the album's lyrics, Angus told rock journalist Murray Engleheart that Bon Scott was a team player in the course of the band's creative process. If he presented the band with a lyric idea they thought could be improved upon, 'you'd say to him, "Bon, you can do better than that," and he would. He'd go away and really work on it, or if he got stuck he'd come and get Mal and say, "Mal, come and bail me out." Mal would help him, give him a few lines or an idea and then he'd flow away or he'd ask me if I had any dirty poetry anywhere! Some inspiration.'

In laying down the album's lead and rhythm guitar tracks, Angus revealed to Masino that, unlike on future albums, 'Mal played solos on four tracks from our first album, when the two of us had traded off. Mal is a good soloist. He can probably do what I do quite well. He plays lead like he would play rhythm, and that doesn't sound like someone else. When we used to trade licks, it was always the same way. He's a very good performer, the heart of the band. I sit and watch him play rhythm, and I go, "Ah, I'll play that now." I'll try to copy what he is doing.'

Even so, when it came to defining the brothers' roles within the band, Angus told *Guitar Player* that, from day one, 'Mal has always pushed me out there in the front. He has always been supportive of what I do and my playing. He would be the first to turn around and say, "Ah, Angus can play. He can do that."'

In refining the album's songs, Angus explained to *Guitar Player* that 'in the early days, if you were playing an A chord, you might play a solo in A; but then again put in progressions or notes in there that don't sound right. It sounds like you're playing in the wrong key or something, and sometimes it works.'

Original AC/DC bassist Mark Evans added to *Undercover Media* that, once Angus, Malcolm and Bon had the basics of a song tracked, 'George Young fine-tuned things. George is an absolute genius. I have never met a more astute person in the studio than George.'

Where drums for any album's songs were concerned, beat-keeper Phil Rudd – in an interview with *Musician* magazine – recalled that right from the start the band kept to a basic formula where 'simplicity has always been the most important thing. The attention to getting everything out of that simple thing… When I get down to business I always revert back to the style that I prefer, which is straight-ahead. Someone said once that I get to play the way that every schoolboy wishes he could play. I don't know what that means, but I agree with it. It is just a foot-tapping thing. I am not out to impress anyone. I am just out to get the job done.'

Elaborating on the Vanda/Young approach to producing records, engineer Mark Opitz – who would become the pair's apprentice – recalled, 'Harry and George ran a very tight little family. While working for Vanda/Young, I learned that, obviously, attitude is a very important thing, but more importantly what I really learned from those guys is you have to be able to tap your foot to it, which is dancing basically. It's got to be able to affect you in that physical sense, whether it's AC/DC or a pop group, you find yourself moving to it. That was one of the prerequisites after you had a melody, which was another one they always emphasised as really important. Melody and feel, probably in that order, is what I really learned from them.'

On *High Voltage*'s local release on Albert Records in Australia, *Billboard* put it on their 'Recommended LPs' list, commenting, 'Australia's newest entry is a cross between Led Zeppelin and the Sensational Alex Harvey Band. Lead singer has a unique-sounding voice, and the twin guitars are front and centre from the first cut. Expect airplay.'

Years later staff producer Chris Gilbey told Masino with a chuckle that 'the album went on to become an even bigger hit without the song "High Voltage" on it! And by the time we had sold a load of albums we were ready to release the next full-length, which did have the song on it, but of course had a different name and that second album was an instant hit. Amazing hit!'

The national success of *High Voltage* led to the band touring extensively throughout their native country, as well as making numerous appearances on *Countdown* – Australia's *American Bandstand*. Keen to build on that success, the band quickly re-entered the studio in July 1975 to record *T.N.T.*, their second LP. It was on this album that Harry Vanda felt AC/DC made their first real progress in establishing their signature sound. 'I suppose there might have been one or two tracks on the first album, a few things that they were experimenting with, which probably later on they wouldn't have done any more,' he told Masino. 'So I suppose you could say that *T.N.T.* was the one that really pulled the identity – like, "This is AC/DC, there's no doubt about it, that's who it's going to be and that's how it's going to stay." Once you know an identity, then you know what not to do.'

In the studio after touring for almost six straight months, the band was a far more seasoned unit, building on what was and would remain their bedrock recording principle – to track together live off the floor. 'A lot of songs we'd try a few takes and most of the time gravitate to the first couple,' Vanda recalled to Masino. 'There was always that sort of immediate, spontaneous thing. They all used to be together in one room anyway – all the amps were lumped in one room with the drums! I suppose it was a recording nightmare, but it worked.'

In harnessing Angus's electric guitar solos, which *Brave Words / Bloody Knuckles* magazine called 'raw, riotous and righteous all in one', the guitarist recalled in an interview with *Gibson* that, during tracking, 'My elder brother George used to always say, "No, don't do that now. Stop." He'd keep me cool and calm until it was time for the guitar solo. Then he'd say, "Now!"'

Revealing the essence of the band's sound underneath his blistering solos, Angus explained to *Gibson* that 'the two of us combine to sound like one big guitar'. But, as well as the brothers got along in the course of creating that magic, Angus did concede in *Guitar Player* that, in the studio, sometimes 'we squabble, but we come together in the music thing. We may have different interpretations of what we do… [and] we'll sit and battle away … but we both know at the end of the day that it's the result that counts… but we probably get along better playing than we would if we were simply living together.'

The band's first hit singles, including 'High Voltage' and the seminal 'It's a Long Way to the Top (If You Wanna Rock 'n' Roll)', introduced AC/DC to the world as a hard-rock band on their way to crafting what would soon become the sonic bedrock for the hard-rock genre they were co-creating along with their only real stylistic competitor, US rockers Aerosmith. Inspired by tireless months on the road, Angus — in an interview with rock journalist Paul Stenning — recalled that the latter song was a natural extension of Bon Scott 'always writing down stuff as he went along, like "Long Way to the Top". George would look through his book. One day George spied the line "A long way to the top if you wanna rock 'n' roll".'

In an interview with Masino, original bassist Mark Evans recalled that the song in its final album form had been edited down from a much lengthier jam. 'The song was never played in one piece in the studio — it was all cut together from one big jam. That was George Young — the guy is a genius.'

As Vanda recalled to Masino, when the band listened back to the final radio/album mix — featuring bagpipes by the multi-talented Bon Scott — 'everyone in the room couldn't help but feel that "Long Way to the Top" was just a great blow. We're all going, "Shit a brick — listen to this!"'

Of the inspiration for 'The Jack', which would become a staple of the band's live tours for decades, Malcolm told rock journalist Murray Engleheart that it was a case of art imitating life: 'We were staying in a big house at the time. If I remember, it was Jimmy Barnes and Cold Chisel, all those guys… We were having a sing-along with the guitars and I got this note from this chick in Melbourne accusing me of giving her a dose of the clap or the jack, and I never had it. So I thought, "Hang on a minute, this chick's fucking given it to me then, if anything!" So I went down to the clinic and I was cleared. But the thing was, when I got the note I gave it to Bon who was sitting next to me and I just started playing a blues and we started together, "She's got the jack…" We sort of threw it away and didn't worry about it, but then a couple of days later we just had a jam with it with the guys, a slow blues, and Bon started singing it again. That song just evolved out of that, really.'

Angus told the same journalist, 'When we first made ['The Jack'] in the studio, they were saying, "Well, maybe we should do two [mixes] because it's a hooky song and maybe the radio might pick it up." So Bon said, "Great, now I can really be clever with it."'

The album's second example of true-life inspiration for Bon's lyrics was another fan classic, 'She's Got Balls' – allegedly written about Scott's soon-to-be ex-wife. As Angus told Stenning, 'Irene had complained to Bon that he'd never written a song about her, so he wrote "She's Got Balls" and she left him! When he joined us she told him, "Bon, it's either them or me." He said, "Well, they're a good band…"'

Celebrating the racy sense of humour that ran through the band's lyrics, Angus explained to Engleheart that 'that was (Bon's) greatness. He called it toilet poetry but it definitely was an art form and he took pride in that.'

When attention turned to crafting the lyrics for the album's title track, Angus told writer Arnaud Durieux that it was very much a group effort. 'We had the title for it – "T.N.T.". But when we were doing the lyrics, Bon came in and said, "I'm getting stuck with this chorus." I was in the back there, chanting along, and George said, "What are you doing?" I said, "Just chanting along." He said, "Why don't you hop out and do what you're doing there? Try it." So it started from that. Then George said it'd be a great intro too, with that going and then Bon coming in. So it was a case of experimenting. I was never the greatest background singer in the world, so George said, "Hey, this is more your cup of tea."'

Released in Australia on December 1975, 'T.N.T.' became a smash hit, making AC/DC overnight rock stars in their own country. 'They played it on the radio and all of a sudden we had what the Easybeats had when we were kids – all the women outside the house. And inside!' Malcolm recalled in *Mojo*. 'Everything was taken care of: there'd be a knock on the door at three in the morning and a bunch of waitresses just off work would be there with bottles of booze, a bag of dope and everything else. Never a dull moment. The cops used to come around because of the noise and smell the dope, but they let us alone. They'd just go, "Oh, can I have a go on the drums?" You name it, it happened in that house. We were poor but living like kings!'

Live, the band was just as powerful as on record, as concert reviewer Rob Tognoni recalled in a Tasmania 1975 review. 'The *T.N.T.* album had been released and "Long Way to the Top" was charting well. After school we headed down to the local basketball centre where the gig was. A local support band called Lava was set up in front of the main stage doing their thing. The occasional "We want AC/DC!!" was hurled at the band, but they played on to finish their set, trying to ignore the obvious impatience of the crowd. After Lava, there was a break of 30 minutes or so with electricity starting to generate in the air. Then it exploded with a voice over the PA: "Ladies and Gentlemen… AC/DC!"'

'Well, the shock that you could have seen on my face and the faces of everyone in the place when the first glimpse of Angus, silhouetted by an intense strobe behind him, launched into "High Voltage" would have been a sight. We had *never* heard such incredible VOLUME before. I made my way to the front row and stood in stunned disbelief at what I was witnessing. All I could think was "FAAARRRK!!!!"'

'Bon leered from stage left, clutching the microphone in one hand and stretching the cable looped in the other. Even as I am writing this I am getting a shiver down my spine …

The mischievous smile, the stance, the little dance – all the legendary Bon Scott trademarks were unfolding in front of me. "Can I Sit Next To You Girl", "I'm A Rocker", "T.N.T.", "She's Got the Jack" – it was relentless with the occasional "You's right? Yas 'avin' a good time…" put to us, which sent us into hoarse screams of "AC/DC – rock 'n' roll!" Then it was "It's a Long Way to the Top" with Bon blowing the living guts out of the bagpipes and finishing with a wall of Marshall white noise, then silence, literal silence for a few seconds – everyone was totally blown away. Then the eruption of applause was nearly equally as deafening as those Marshalls were…'

AC/DC soon made enough noise to catch the attention of Atlantic Records, who signed the band in spring 1976. The label quickly combined tracks from *T.N.T.* and the band's debut LP, *High Voltage*, and chose the latter as the title for the band's international LP debut. 'They had signed us in '76, so our record company felt if they put a combination of those two records together it would be a good introduction,' Angus told *Brave Words/Bloody Knuckles* years later.

The new *High Voltage* included much of *T.N.T.*'s content, with the final track listing being: 'It's a Long Way to the Top (If You Wanna Rock 'n' Roll)', 'Rock 'n' Roll Singer', 'The Jack', 'Live Wire', 'T.N.T.', 'Can I Sit Next to You Girl', 'Little Lover', 'She's Got Balls' and 'High Voltage'.

Released internationally on 14 May 1976, the album

announced AC/DC's arrival with such singular force that, decades later — well after the album had been certified triple platinum — *Billboard* magazine would look back and hail *High Voltage* as 'the blueprint' for a rock sub-genre the band would pioneer and shape over the next three decades, adding that the record possessed 'every single one of AC/DC's archetypes'. *Blender* magazine, meanwhile, would single out such cuts as 'Live Wire' and 'T.N.T.' as making for 'a spectacularly noisy calling card'. Similarly, *Brave Words/Bloody Knuckles* magazine would rank the album as 'a top-notch nugget that personifies the band and Scott's electrifying presence', declaring that 'it ain't a party until this gets cranked!'

Recorded at the same furious pace as the band performed many of its blazing numbers, *Dirty Deeds Done Dirt Cheap*, AC/DC's third studio album in less than three years as a group, would mark the sign of a band steadily on the rise, inspiring *Billboard* to conclude that it had a 'supercharged, nervy pulse', and 'there's a real sense of danger to this record'. That sentiment was precisely what the band was going for as they headed into recording. Bon Scott reasoned at the time that — consistent with the band's broader style — 'songs might change. Just as long as the balls are there, the rock balls. And that's what's important to us.'

Still, while the band wanted it known that the music they

played was ballsy, Malcolm later took the opportunity in an interview with *Mojo* to clarify that 'we're not like some macho band. We take the music far more seriously than we take the lyrics ... Once you've got the music, the titles sort of write themselves.' That said, he went out of his way to highlight Bon's genius as a lyricist, reasoning that 'Chuck Berry was the master when it comes to lyrics – even John Lennon said he was the best lyric writer in rock 'n' roll. He would sing about sex in the back seat in such a way that it was funny – if we came out with a song like "Sweet Little Sixteen" they'd probably arrest us. That and Little Richard's sense of humour with words – and of course Bon. We just try to come somewhere near the area that those guys have all been.'

In composing the music for those lyrics, Malcolm spoke of a spontaneous style. 'Back then we never went into the studio with anything more than a riff,' he told Masino. 'In fact, we thought a riff was a song. Fortunately, we had the producers there to turn them into songs and it's been pretty much the same ever since. Back then we really didn't know any better.'

Where Angus's leads for the album were concerned, producer George placed an equal emphasis on the moment, with Angus recalling that 'you got it into your head whenever you went in the studio that you always tried to get it all in one take. It has to flow. Solos have got to have continuity.'

Released in November 1976, *Dirty Deeds Done Dirt Cheap*'s title track gave AC/DC one of their biggest hits of the 1970s as they continued to write hard rock's soundtrack. In its retrospective assessment years later, *Billboard* said, 'More than most of their songs to date, it captured the seething malevolence of Bon Scott, the sense that he *revelled* in doing bad things, encouraged by the maniacal riffs of Angus and Malcolm Young, who provided him with their most brutish rock 'n' roll yet.' Upon its reissue in the US in April 1981 (following the monster back-to-back successes of *Highway to Hell* and *Back in Black*), the album would debut at No. 3 on the Billboard Top 200 Album Chart, proving their growing fan base was equally appreciative of any musical era of the band.

CHAPTER THREE

LET THERE BE ROCK
(1977)

'We know what we are… rock 'n' roll'
ANGUS YOUNG

AC/DC got to the heart of their musical matter on 1977's *Let There Be Rock*. In the opening lines of the title track, Bon Scott narrated the creation of hard rock in the same Biblical style as that of the world in Genesis, and through the band's music the genre of hard rock was experiencing its own explosion into life.

Angus described to *Mojo* how he expressed the band's desire to make a 'guitar' album to brother George. '[He'd] asked us what kind of album we wanted to make and we said it would be great if we could just make a lot of guitar riffs, because we were all fired up after doing all this touring.' Years later in a conversation with rock journalist Murray Engleheart, he added that, heading into the studio, the group consensus had been: 'We said, "we'll just make a fucking good guitar album! Fuck it!"'

LET THERE BE ROCK (1977)

Embodying the live energy of a band who had their own brand of frenzy in their playing style, Malcolm elaborated to *Metal CD*, 'I suppose we were a bit more serious and we wanted to get a rawer sound and cut out the commercial choruses like "T.N.T.".' We knew exactly what we wanted, which was to have three really strong live tracks to flesh out the set. "Whole Lotta Rosie" we knew would be a sure-fire winner, and "Bad Boy Boogie" and "Let There Be Rock" were the other two we felt would really go the distance on stage. Those three have really overshadowed most of the other songs on the album and ended up in the live set for years after.'

Let There Be Rock was knocked out in a quick few weeks of recording in January and February 1977. Looking back, Malcolm described to Engleheart how the band was in a generally creative groove at that point. 'We could go in in the old days, set up the kit and the amps, be in there two hours and bang, we're knocking out tracks. We used to come in from the gigs – we'd work five or six gigs a week – finishing at about two in the morning, then drive down to the studio. George and Harry would have a couple of dozen cans in and a few bottles of Jack Daniel's and we'd all get in and have a party and rip it up, get the fast tracks – stuff like "Whole Lotta Rosie" and "Let There Be Rock" – done right so it was the same loose feeling like we were still on stage. The studio was just like an extension of the gig back then.'

From a production perspective, co-producer Harry Vanda explained to Engleheart how, with AC/DC, 'spontaneous is basically the word. I suppose if we were talking at the time about no-bullshit rock 'n' roll, we meant it! Balls everywhere! Not like the Americans' no-bullshit rock 'n' roll, which takes two years to record. [The band] had very, very definite ideas what it is they wanted to be. And so did we.'

'In that field, you're always looking for bigger and better bass drums, bigger and better snare drums, and as a result everything comes up with it. We never worried that much about whether things were that correct as sounds. To us, it was always more important whether it had the balls and the atmosphere – you know, whether it had the heart. So if we had to choose between a take which had all the heart and it was farting and buzzing and all that, we'd go for that, because we'd prefer that to the sterile version, which might have been correct but it was boring. On *Let There Be Rock*, we managed to marry a few of those things where the sound was good as well, plus the performances were all there.'

On another occasion, he confirmed this approach to rock writer Susan Masino: 'We tried to capture that energy they had onstage. You had to get them at the right time, when they were really fired up.'

Having stepped out more aggressively on lead solos than he had in the past, Angus explained Malcolm was 'the one that shoved me in the first place. He got me into it: "I want you to do all of this." In the early days we used to fool around on some of our first albums. He would do little bits of guitar. We would double up, swap, do a solo here, a solo there. Malcolm's more experienced at it than me … He knows what he's doing with it. He's got his own style and his own sound.'

Expanding on the duo's creative process in the studio, Angus said, 'There's many a time we'll get in there – and we might even be in the middle of a song – and we'll just stop and put a tape on if somebody's got a blow [improvisation] or something. All of our early material was basically written in the studio. We got in there and did "Let There Be Rock", "Whole Lotta Rosie", most of them. We used to go in with a few ideas, and then really do the big per cent of it in the studio – arrange it and everything. In the early days we didn't even rehearse. Nowadays we try to save time. We don't like spending too much time in the studio. We get the band together in rehearsals, try and get as many songs as possible, and then take them into the studio.'

Of the creation of 'Whole Lotta Rosie' – which would become a live favourite for Guns N' Roses as well as an AC/DC concert staple – Angus began by explaining to Engleheart that, from a musical – and specifically rhythmic – vantage point, 'We were always big fans of early rock 'n' roll, like Elvis and "Heartbreak Hotel", things like that – the stop-and-start things, the dynamics. If anything, for "Whole Lotta Rosie" we were looking for a feel like Little Richard – a good old steamin' rock feel – and see what we could lay on top with the guitars. It evolved into that, but you're just looking for the vibe, what's exciting, and that's what we were listening to. Simple to put together, but still around like a classic.'

Angus also told Masino that initially 'Malcolm had the guitar riff and George said, "Why don't we try a little bit of an experiment, try inserting these breaks at the front of the song?"'

From a lyrical perspective, lead vocalist Bon Scott explained that – as so often in his autobiographical style of writing – the inspiration behind Rosie was again a case of art imitating life. 'I woke up in the morning and to get out of bed I had to climb over her, which was like climbing a mountain. I stopped halfway for a rest and, before I knew it, I was balling her again.'

Angus would confirm to Masino that 'Bon wrote that song about a huge Tasmanian woman he had shared a "wild time" with in Melbourne. Interestingly, the band ran into her again in Hobart, Tasmania, but she had lost a lot of weight and Bon was disappointed that she was no longer the 42-39-56 that he remembered. She did know the song was about her, and took it as a compliment.'

Tour manager Ian Jeffery shed some additional light on

Scott's lyrical writing process to Engleheart. 'The lyrics were sketchy but that's the way Bon did it. It was like a little notebook that he'd flip over and make a few notes, scribble one or two lines, cross them out, add one thing – sometimes one word would change – or he'd write two words on one page. Bon was quite organised. He had a folder with all [his potential lyrics] inside. Believe it or not, Bon used to come to work with a folder and he'd leave with it – that was his life. That was Bon. And he'd have postcards in there that he was writing to people. He was the best communicator in the world.'

By the end of the album, Scott was delighted with the vocals he'd laid over an instrumental album he was equally pleased with. 'Things fall into place sometimes,' he mused in an interview with *Countdown*.

Angus added to the *Countdown* interviewer that, while recording *Let There Be Rock*, the band had rocked up such a storm that 'towards the end, the fucking amp was smoking – there was smoke pouring out of the back of the fucking amp! George is fucking screaming, "Don't stop!" I'm there fucking banging away and I could see this fucking smoke filling up the fucking room. It lasted until the end and then this fucking amp, it was just like it gave in – it was just "Blaaah!" It melted. [That] was an album where it was cooking!'

Angus would later recall to *Brave Words/Bloody Knuckles* feeling 'very proud of the *Let There Be Rock* album, especially

Malcolm and myself, because for the first time we could really feature the guitars!'

Let There Be Rock was released worldwide on 23 June 1977, featuring a cover – a mock-Biblical epic movie still – that appropriately showed the band live onstage, reflecting the energy of the record. Years later Angus would credit it as 'the album that kicked it home for us all over the world'. Having immediately gone gold, it went on to sell more than two million copies before the end of the decade. Fans were going crazy for AC/DC.

Let There Be Rock was a definite step forward in the eyes of everyone. *Billboard* hailed the album for being 'as lean and mean as the original line-up ever got', while Antimusic.com declared it 'an instant AC/DC classic'. *Blender* magazine noted that 'AC/DC cranked up the volume and intensity, making this weightier than their earlier albums' but it was *Billboard* who hit the nail on the head. 'Shaved down to the bone, there are only eight tracks, giving [*Let There Be Rock*] a lethal efficiency … It has a bit of a bluesier edge than other AC/DC records, but this is truly the sound of the band reaching its peak.'

CHAPTER FOUR

POWERAGE (1978)

'Our albums are all rock 'n' roll'
BON SCOTT

With their fifth album, *Powerage*, AC/DC announced their arrival on rock's main stage. The celebratory opening album anthem 'Rock 'n' Roll Damnation' let the world know that the band was on the brink of changing rock 'n' roll forever, offering listeners the chance to escape while they still had a choice.

In spite of that warning, the rock universe seemed happily possessed by a sound that *Blender* would report made *Powerage* 'Keith Richards's favourite AC/DC album'. Angus told rock journalist Paul Stenning that he 'always thought that album set us apart from a lot of other bands', while Malcolm declared to rock journalist Murray Engleheart, 'I think that's the most under-rated album of them all.' It was a sentiment that would be echoed by MTV, who years later would say *Powerage* was among the band's most 'overlooked' achievements.

POWERAGE (1978)

For the band's final collaboration in the Bon Scott era with the Vanda/Young production team, Malcolm added that the band made a conscious decision to stick with the same sonic formula that had defined their previous four albums. 'That album was more of the same,' he explained to Metal CD. 'We were happy to stay in the same area as *Let There Be Rock* because all that stuff was going down so well on stage.'

The only changes to the band's approach to working in the studio came the arrivals of engineer Mark Opitz and new bassist Cliff Williams, who had replaced original member Mark Evans. In an interview with *Guitar School*, Williams recalled that, when he auditioned, the band was looking to strengthen their rhythm section, so they'd come to London where there was a larger pool of players. 'They had a few records out at that point, were successful in Australia and toured Europe once or twice, but hadn't been to the States yet. They were looking to tour the US behind the *Let There Be Rock* album. Anyway, I got a call from a friend of a friend who thought I might be right for the job, and I ended up auditioning a number of times.'

Ironically, though he toured the States with the band, the bassist had a harder time getting Down Under to start recording, as engineer Mark Opitz recalled. '*Powerage* was very interesting, because we spent about three weeks in rehearsals. Cliff had just joined the band, didn't have his visa yet and couldn't get into Australia for a little bit. So we went into the other studio, which we never used, at around 8 or 9 at night, and would play till 5 or 6 in the morning, with George Young playing bass. Harry and I would be in the control room, working out the songs.'

While Vanda and Young were hard at work with the band fleshing out the album's songs, Opitz was working just as diligently to take advantage of that interval. 'I went through every Marshall amplifier and speaker box, and tested each amp against not only each box, but each speaker. I did that every day until I came up with what I thought was the right amp top and right speaker box for Malcolm, and the right amp top and right speaker box for Angus. They were J&P Marshalls with Celestion speakers. I remember I had a notebook where I cross-referenced everything I liked until I matched everything up. That's how we did the whole record, and we had great amps and speaker matches.'

The result, as *Stylus* magazine would later describe in its review of *Powerage*, was 'indeed about power... electrical power, power chords and a band at the peak of their powers'.

Part of the creation of that power came courtesy of what Angus described in an interview with *Guitar Player* as 'this big, giant custom amp that Marshall built us at their factory. I think it rates about 350 watts. Then I've got about eight 100-watt Marshalls up there, but I think they only use four at once. We mike the amps [during recording]; there's nothing direct except the bass. They take a DI [direct input] for the bass.'

Just prior to entering Albert Studios to track *Powerage*, newly added assistant engineer Colin Abrahams recalled that 'shortly after the installation of the new MCI JH-500 console in Studio 2, AC/DC came into that studio several times to try it out. They did several sessions in that studio but they did not like it as much as Studio 1. Studio 1 had a much more open live recording room than Studio 2, which was heavily damped and had a drum hut. Studio 1 remained the "rock 'n' roll" studio where most of the in-house Alberts artists recorded, whilst Studio 2 became the "high tech" studio where most of the outside work was done, including many other major Australian bands signed to other record companies, major commercial productions, Australian country and religious music.'

'AC/DC was in and out of the studios quite a lot at that time. Usually, the entire band was there. I was called in at one stage to look at some problem with the gear in Studio 1 and was introduced to the entire band. Bon went out of his way to be friendly and insisted that I stayed for a beer – life's tough in some jobs! Being the junior engineer, I did not have a lot to do with AC/DC directly. Most of the engineering was done by Mark Opitz, under the watchful eye of Vanda and Young.'

Opitz recalled, 'Albert Studios had two main studios. One was just our studio – Harry, George and I – and that housed a Neve console, which was a great console. I'd been lucky because, prior to that, I'd gotten to work on the Abbey Road console at EMI, and then I was working with the classic Neve. The other studio ... had an MCI J500, but we had

36

Above: Lock up your daughters: from left, Malcolm Young, Mark Evans, Bon Scott, Angus Young and Phil Rudd. © *Rex Features*

Below: The Easybeats were an early influence on AC/DC. © *Rex Features*

Angus Young at his mid-70s peak.
© Rex Features

Above: AC/DC out on the town with, far left, Bon Scott fooling around.

Below: Malcolm and Angus Young together in 1976.

Bon Scott in a break during rehearsals.

© *Rex Features*

Above: Live in late 1980.

Below: AC/DC with Brian Johnson.

The bronze statue of Bon Scott unveiled in 2008.　　　© *Rex Features*

Above: Geordie in 1973 with, far left, a pre-AC/DC Brian Johnson.

© *Getty Images*

Below: Brian Johnson's AC/DC stage gear.

© *Getty Images*

Phil Rudd with Angus Young just behind him. © *Rex Features*

classic Neve, which was beautiful and what we recorded all the AC/DC stuff on. There was a third, separate room where I put all the guitar amps. I used two Phet U 47 Neumann microphones – not the valve ones, but the transistor ones – and put a 10DB pad on the mic so it could take the pressure of the source, and then picked the spots where the speakers sounded best around the room, again through research. And miked them each from a distance of maybe a foot, and that was that.

'They laid the rhythm tracks down as a band. The solos were overdubbed, but everything else went down straight. There wasn't anything piecemeal about it – you did it that way because you needed to catch the feel. So, by having both Angus and Malcolm's guitars in the same room, I had the speaker boxes back to back, which meant you had an extreme left and right in the same room. So any spill would work out in the mix as natural, but still give you the full left and right so you can get that sonic separation you need.

'For the miking of the amps, because I had Malcolm's right hand playing over heavy-gauge strings, those valve amps would power right up, and, with the pre-amps, we could get the harmonic distortion right up there without blowing the speakers out. Malcolm was playing a Gretsch, which is traditionally a loud pick-up guitar, and those 10-52 strings he was using, turning the amp up without over-choking it when you're striking, it gets very big and loud. Malcolm is a little guy but, as a rhythm guitar player, he drives the band. He is AC/DC no question.'

Angus agreed with the engineer's assessment, telling rock journalist Paul Cashmere, 'I admire my brother Malcolm. The rhythm playing and good rhythm guitarists are a dying species. There is not many of them coming up in this new style music world. The great ones are Keith Richards and Ike Turner. They are great rhythm players.'

Angus added in an interview with *Guitar Player* that the siblings' unique style of guitar-duelling was at times deceptive because 'Malcolm plays a lot with his fingers. He does a lot of picking. It's part of the rhythm ... I do play with me fingers but you can't see it ... The two of us always slap the guitar.'

Indeed, *Circus* magazine noted in their review that '*Powerage* shows AC/DC to have evolved ... to full blown competence' and credited that 'mainly to Angus and his brother Malcolm, who maintain a deliciously fat and nasty two-guitar sound throughout the album'.

Giving an insight into the way the brothers worked within the band, engineer Mark Opitz explained that Angus and Malcolm had been really young when AC/DC first started. 'Angus was still in school and Malcolm wasn't, so, even though there's a couple of years age difference, that's a massive difference when you're young. Malcolm was the big brother of Angus, and he put the band together with his brother George. George and Malcolm are the sort of people who can look at stuff and make it move by looking at it – they have that sort of determination, just naturally. You can hear it in the music, that's just Malcolm – working class, bang, in your face, here it is. So pretty much all the time, Malcolm would be the driving force inside the band – Malcolm ruled, no question. The band would look to him for cues and changes as the band played live together.

'That said, from what Malcolm does foundationally, Angus as a player is more emotive, because he's got more blues in his playing. That's why his solos are blues-feeling and single-note. The guy never had a guitar out of his hand when he was in the studio basically – a cigarette and guitar.'

Elaborating further on Angus's gifts as a lead player, co-producer Vanda explained to journalist Engleheart, 'Angus has got a talent for … those flowing rock riffs … If you write a riff you better go check with Angus, because chances are he'll already have one exactly like that.'

As usual the band tracked live off the floor at Albert Studios. 'The way it worked,' Opitz recalled of their recording routine, 'was we'd sit around the studio control room – because we also recorded very late at night – and Malcolm would walk in and toss everyone a cigarette. It was funny: whenever he was lighting up a cigarette, he'd toss one to each of us. And that was kind of customary, so you had to come in with two packs of cigarettes, because every time you had a cigarette you had to slide a cigarette to everyone else in the band.

'And we'd sit around and talk, and all of a sudden we'd pick on something –it might be "What about that TV guy?" – and, once we were into the discussion, George would say "OK, let's go and do a take." And it would go bang, bang, bang – two or three takes and done. We kept doing it that way, and then, after a period of time, came back and revisited it. "OK, what about that song we did three nights ago? We can do it better now," and we'd go about correcting each song until we had a keeper take. Then we'd look at getting the solos done.'

'A lot of them wouldn't have lyrics yet, and Bon would be in there – just going along with the feel, because all of the lyrics came from feel. And then some sort of simple melody would be added, and the words would come along later.'

Describing himself as 'the poet of the band', Bon brought his strongest lyrical writing yet to *Powerage*. As *Stylus* magazine attested, it has 'the "more" factor; it has cleverer than average lyrics and … substance… With *Powerage*, Bon's lifeblood (sex, booze, rock 'n' roll) is mixed bitterly and savagely with the painful decline of his marriage in a series of songs that string together sodden metaphors and wordplay to create a dark grindhouse movie about a man who dreams feverishly of getting even with his woman. And with their meatiest and most inspired performances ever, the band creates the perfect soundtrack to Bon's jaded journey into the dead of night…'

'No stranger to hard times, Bon came from a bona fide working-class background, spent some time in juvenile hall and didn't begin making decent money at music until he was in his thirties. Hence, when Bon sings for working-class solidarity in the fast and nimble "Riff Raff", it scorches with fire-lunged sincerity. An enthralling hard-rock epic, "Down Payment Blues" finds Bon criss-crossing financial hardship ("hiding from the rent man" etc.) with fragile dreams of luxury; easily his best lyrics, the last verse is especially impressive.'

In one interview Bon credited his songwriting inspiration as coming 'from life on the road really. Whatever comes into my brain when we're on the road I jot down on a tape recorder, in order not to lose it. Usually I'm in a drunken state; when I listen back to it the next morning I think, "Hey, did I say that? Did I think that?" But out of it you can usually get some pretty good road stuff.'

The Young brothers openly expressed their appreciation of Bon's role in the band, with Malcolm explaining to *Mojo* that 'with Bon, that's when the band became a band. With Bon we had a real character in the band with his own style and his own idea for lyrics.'

Extending that creative dynamic into the studio, Opitz explained that 'everyone had their role to play in the band. Malcolm was the rhythm guitarist: "I'm laying it down." Angus: "You're the lead player, you come up with the solo." Bon: "You're the singer, you come up with the words." That was it. That was Bon's responsibility, lyrics. When he'd finish a set of lyrics, he'd take them to George and Harry, and they'd go through them, along with Malcolm.'

'George had his hand on the rudder, most definitely. In the earlier records I hadn't been involved in, he was running the ship, co-writing, and that's why they sounded a lot poppier in the beginning. By the time I came along, it was more 50/50. The guys would be writing the songs and George would be in there suggesting stuff, still running the ship but trying to give them their legs as well at the same time. By that stage of their career, they were four albums in, and Malcolm and Angus had grown very much into their own as writers, along of course with Bon.'

Expanding on George Young and Harry Vanda's roles in the band's record-making process, Opitz said of George Young that 'the bedside manner was something that would have been honed over a generation, because he's the older brother of both of them. With any Vanda and Young production, you've also got the soul and the heart that they bring out in their recordings. George is the heart and Harry is the soul, and their personalities really come through in the records they make. George, like Angus and Malcolm, is more hard-ass – sort of go for it, try to make it work – where Harry's more laid-back, feel-oriented – the emotive side. They'd started off as a writing team, and had been writing songs for people in the '70s, as well as with AC/DC on the side. The primary function of Albert Productions at that time was making hits for unknown singers, which they also produced as a team. So, if you listen to AC/DC, as they went on, that pop element of AC/DC got less and less over those albums, and *Powerage* was a real turning point.'

As for his own contribution, Opitz – whose experience in television and record production included becoming EMI Records Australia's staff producer before the age of 21– quipped that 'what I think I brought to the table was basically wonderment, amazement – have I bitten off more than I can chew? Most of all, I was just stoked overall to be there while you're doing a track like "Riff Raff", sitting at the console with Angus thumping into the back of my chair because he was doing his solo in the control room.

'Because I'd been working at EMI studios in that producer/engineer role, I was working with Richard Lush, who had worked with the Beatles as either an assistant or engineer on all their stuff, and at EMI we had Abbey Road consoles. One area I focused on improving when I first started working with them was that their miking techniques were very rudimentary. I think one of the things I brought to the party was miking techniques, and if you listen to something like *Powerage*, as against the earlier records, it's pretty obvious. There's a change in the guitar sounds, and the clarity's improved. Where they'd previously been using whatever mic was lying around, because of my training at ABC TV and EMI, I pretty much knew what everything did.

It was always a passion for me to get into the magic of what I was doing, including with miking. Vanda and Young as producers were coming from a pure songwriting point of view, where I came from a sonic landscape point of view – as well as music arrangement.'

Rounding out that sonic landscape were Phil Rudd's powering drums, which, Opitz recalled, came from him 'playing on a Sonor drum kit, and the room we were recording it was pretty much a rectangular room, not even four foot by twenty foot. So I pretty much had the drums coming out of one corner of the room. I started out miking the snare with a KM-64 pencil mic, but then switched pretty quickly to the Sennheiser 441 on the top of the snare, which I liked because the Sennheiser 441 has a longer, dynamic microphone, has anti-face tubing on the front, so it projects lots more and is more directional. I would have miked the snare underneath with an RE-20, on the toms, and I would have used Neumann U-87s on overheads.'

'For Bon's vocals, we used a U-47 Neumann going into the Neve 1073 mic-pre, and then into that big, fat box compressor that's in the desk and then straight to tape.' The two grew to trust one another on both a creative and personal level in the course of making the album, and Opitz recounted a humorous incident late in the vocal tracking. 'I can remember one night Bon came up to me and said, "Hey, mate, do you have anything to smoke?" And I asked, "What do you mean?" And he said,

"I've got to go and write lyrics tonight." I remember giving him a tiny little bit of hash, and off he went. The kicker to that was six months later, he came back from an American tour and tracked me down. He had this *massive* amount of hash on him, broke it in two and gave half to me!'

As recording neared its end, the band – at the urging of their label Atlantic – went back into the studio at short notice to come up with a single with which the label could launch the band on American radio. The result became one of the album's biggest hits, 'Rock 'n' Roll Damnation'. As Opitz recalled, 'They weren't too impressed with having to go back into the studio to do another song. Integrity was pretty much what these guys were trying to establish all the time, and I had that feeling that, while we were doing "Rock 'n' Roll Damnation", which was a late addition because we knew we didn't have a single yet. We had these great tracks, but there wasn't a radio track, so that was an afterthought. That would have been more George really stepping up to the plate in crafting that song. George and Harry would have taken a more major role in adding things like maracas, and things like that. It was obvious the song "Rock 'n' Roll Damnation" was a hit.'

The other big hit off *Powerage* was 'Sin City' – a song that *Stylus* magazine called 'the black heart of the album' and 'the strongest song in the entire AC/DC catalogue'. Malcolm agreed years later that it 'was the big one on *Powerage*, and we're still getting some mileage out of it when we play it live'.

When attention turned to mixing the album, Opitz explained, 'George and Harry were running the ship, particularly George. The two big things I picked up from them as the goals of mixing an AC/DC record were: a) when I closed my eyes, I could see the band playing, and b) I could hear each instrument as well. That's what was important: getting to that magic moment where one and one equals three – all of a sudden it becomes greater than the sum of its parts.'

Angus shared Opitz's happiness with the overall achievement of *Powerage*. 'I like the album. I think because it has got a good mix for me. You've got rock tunes, but you've got a few things in there that are different.'

Upon its release on 25 May 1978, *Powerage* plugged AC/DC into the international mainstream for the first time in their short three-year career. 'AC/DC does have real power now,' declared *Circus* magazine, '[and it] may be enough to take them to the top of the hard-rock heap.' Years later, *Stylus* would declare *Powerage* 'AC/DC's best album'. Indeed, Malcolm proudly confirmed to journalist Engleheart, 'I know a lot of people respect *Powerage*. A lot of real rock 'n' roll AC/DC fans, the real pure rock 'n' roll guys.'

Elaborating on the band's fiercely loyal and ever-growing fan base, Angus told journalist Paul Stenning that 'back in Australia, we were like your average kid into rock 'n' roll from a small-town background. We were like the outcasts or whatever, always getting into trouble with the cops and picked on because we had long hair and didn't dress like them. But we made it on to the stage and the fans are still trying to get there, or at least dreaming and fantasising about it. We haven't forgotten what it was like and we are definitely on the kids' side.'

The band rounded out the success of *Powerage* with the release of a live album – recorded on tour in front of a legendarily enthusiastic Scottish audience – later that year. In December 1978, *If You Want Blood (You Got It)* brought full circle a sound they'd been honing on the road for years, but first brought to a level of mastery on the 'live off the floor' albums *Let There Be Rock* and *Powerage*. Malcolm – in an interview with *Metal CD* years later – proudly recalled that the live LP reflected 'exactly where we were at that stage in our career. That record summed up the band perfectly and it was recorded at one of the last gigs from that tour, at the Glasgow Apollo.'

Engineer Colin Abrahams described mixing the album: 'I do remember the arrival of the master tapes for the *If You Want Blood* album – I had to do 24-track safety copies before they were mixed down. The tapes came in on massive 15-inch spools. While the tapes were being copied I turned up the faders on the desk to have a listen and check things. The guitar tracks were recorded in pairs with different mic combinations. Each amp had at least one U47 mic on it – sorry, I can't remember what the other mics were. Just playing it back with the faders almost in a straight line, I remember the sound was awesome! There was an unbelievable sense of excitement in those raw recordings. I don't think much was done to them in the mix down – everything was already there. Vanda and Young mixed them down on to four-track (two sets of stereo pairs), to allow overlapping of the applause between songs before finally mixing it down to two-track.'

On its release, the album would fit in perfectly to the live-LP craze that had taken off, with the likes of Ted Nugent's *Double Live Gonzo*, Led Zeppelin's *The Song Remains the Same*, Kiss's *Alive I and II*, Peter Frampton's *Frampton Comes Alive*, Aerosmith's *Double Live Bootleg*, and more. *Classic Rock* magazine would go on to rank AC/DC's *If You Want Blood (You Got It)* among its Top 50 Live Albums of All Time, while *Blender* enthused about how 'the audience's hysteria regularly cuts through the amps, as they howl along to singer Bon Scott's tale of sexually transmitted disease ("The Jack") and punctuate guitarist Angus Young's staccato riffing on "Whole Lotta Rosie". Imagine a punk-rock Chuck Berry played at nosebleed volume.'

If You Want Blood (You Got It) would peak at No. 13 on the UK albums chart and, heading into 1979, the stakes would only get higher for a band well on their way to the top.

CHAPTER FIVE

HIGHWAY TO HELL (1979)

'There was no way we'd back down on anything. We were
a pretty tough band for any producer to work with'
MALCOLM YOUNG

'Somebody asked me … whether they'd remixed
"Highway to Hell" for Iron Man, and we went to see
the movie and, no, they hadn't. It was still the
original mix, which lets me know the sound has
held up all these years'
ENGINEER MARK DEARNLEY

H*ighway to Hell* was AC/DC's shot at a Hard Rock
Heavyweight Championship Title. As *Kerrang!* noted,
following 'a string of shit-kicking, no nonsense hard-
rock albums' that signalled 'the band's global ambitions',
with the *Highway To Hell* album 'they finally broke through
internationally'.

One key to that breakthrough came with the addition to
the team of producer Robert 'Mutt' Lange, a man on the rise
in his own right. In fact, Lange was not the first producer the
band was asked to consider working with in the studio. The
beginning of that journey came when the band's label,

Atlantic, asked the band to part ways with their mainstay production team of Vanda and Young. Being team players, the pair agreed to step aside, a move that manager Michael Browning told rock journalist Murray Engleheart he thought was 'pretty honourable... They could have been outwardly sort of pissed off; I'm sure they were. For an American record company to say to you, "You've got to change producers," when they're sort of revered in their own country was a little bit of a slap in the face, I suppose. So it was very, very difficult. Malcolm and Angus didn't like it at all; they were very pissed off. They were unhappy about it.'

The label next attempted to hook the band up with Eddie Kramer, who had engineered the early Jimi Hendrix studio albums and built Electric Ladyland Studios for him before going on to produce other artists. The attempted pairing was a mismatch from the start as far as the band was concerned. Kramer told Engleheart that his feeling from the get-go was that AC/DC was a very independent bunch. 'They're a simple, raw, basic, to-the-point rock 'n' roll band, a fundamental rock 'n' roll band that is hard to find ... Obviously they were very talented and I thought we could make a really good record here. But I think the problem that I had with it was that the material wasn't quite ready and the way they worked was in a sort of strange manner, I guess. It was kind of, "Oh, we've got these songs," and Bon Scott was having problems with the lyrics and problems with drinking and everything else ... In

50

retrospect, he was such a prototypical tough-guy rocker and his image in terms of drinking and carousing and being completely out of control ... That was his style and I was not used to dealing with that.'

In rebutting the notion that Bon's partying affected his personal life and specifically the studio, Angus explained to rock journalist Paul Stenning that 'he couldn't have recorded albums and stuff if he'd been in the condition they said he was in. When we were touring there may have been six months of the year when he was as dry as a bone and if we got one night off then he was entitled to a drink. Bon was not a heavy drinker.'

Scott's own reply was that the producer 'couldn't produce a healthy fart'.

Homing in on Kramer's own deficiencies, Malcolm Young told Engleheart that 'Eddie, we soon learned, was just a good sound man. He'd get good sounds but he was too... [He] walked in and he played us a Rolling Stones track and he played us another track from someone else and said, "Put that verse together with that chorus and I've got you a hit." We just went, "Fuck off!" That's the end of that, it wasn't going to work out.'

Years later, Malcolm would confirm to *Mojo* that '[Kramer] would interfere a lot and suggest things that were miles from what the band was'.

As for what the band was looking for in a producer, Angus told rock journalist Paul Cashmere that it had to be someone who truly and fully 'got' who the band was. That began with understanding that 'we started life as a band. AC/DC was a band first and foremost. We never looked at ourselves as individual pieces. That has always been the way we have looked at it. I have never said AC/DC is one guitar solo and here is your drum solo. AC/DC is a combination of five guys who all play with the same intent in mind. We go out there to play a bit of rock 'n' roll. We aren't five individual guys displaying their technique.'

Seeking out a replacement who would not attempt to change the band's bottom-line sound in the studio was 'a tricky situation', Malcolm acknowledged to *Mojo* years later. 'The label was going to drop us if we didn't ... We said to our manager, "[Kramer]'s got to go, otherwise you're not going to have a band." He did a bit of wheeling-dealing and got a tape to a friend of his, Mutt Lange.'

Manager Michael Browning told Engleheart, 'I just turned round to Mutt, virtually as I had Malcolm on the phone and said, "Mate, you've got to do this record." That was it.'

By that point Kramer seemed to feel his input as producer would remain fairly limited as 'the two brothers were just really calling the shots'. The band's next step was to ensure his exit, and Malcolm recalled to *Mojo* that this went down when he and Angus simply told him, '"We're having tomorrow off — we need a break." And we went in and wrote nine songs in one day and whacked them off to Mutt. He got straight back and said he wanted to do it.'

To avoid the sort of creative conflict that had arisen with Kramer, the band struck up a compromise of sorts with Lange. As Malcolm explained years later to *Metal CD*, 'He looked after the commercial side while we took care of the riffs and somehow we managed to meet in the middle without feeling as though we compromised ourselves.'

Their next album, by label demand, needed to embody a more radio-friendly feel, and the band quickly sensed this strength in their new studio collaborator. 'Mutt knew what FM stereo sounded like and we didn't,' Angus explained to *Brave Words/Bloody Knuckles*. 'Every week he'd go there with the Top 10 of America, listening to the sounds. And he's got a great set of ears.'

Malcolm added in an interview with *Metal CD* that such a commercial consideration 'was a definite change for AC/DC. Atlantic Records in America were unhappy because they couldn't get the band on the radio and they were desperate for us to come up with something more accessible. We'd had our own way for a few albums, so we figured let's give them what they want and everyone will be happy.'

Lange, for his part, remembered feeling optimistic heading into the collaboration, 'as long as somebody has an interest in working with me and I think their sound is something I can work with'. While the producer had his own sonic picture in mind, he added, 'Angus has a certain vision for his music, which works for him.'

Once the band and Lange were locked, loaded and ready to rock, they entered the famed Roundhouse Studios in London. As engineer Mark Dearnley recalled, 'For *Highway to Hell*, both Mutt and I came into the project fairly last minute. I came off a vacation and back to work not knowing who I was working with, and Mutt at first didn't think he was going to get the gig.'

Having wanted a producer who was sure enough of himself to have a vision for the album without compromising the band's bedrock sound, Malcolm felt that it was an advantage that Lange was still a relative unknown at the time. 'I don't even think at that point that he had even had a big album, a big success,' he told *Brave Words/Bloody Knuckles*. 'I think he'd had a few single successes in this part of the world but he hadn't had a major album and for us it was our first time really working with someone else as a producer. But we felt it was a good combination because we had wanted to try a few different things. Up until that point we had made a lot more in-your-face rock 'n' roll and we wanted to try a couple of medium-style rock tracks.'

Describing the studio, fellow British engineer Trevor Hallesy explained that the Roundhouse was 'the standard session studio, owned by Bronze Records, and originally designed for their own artists like Uriah Heep, and mainstream pop artists like that who were signed to the label. This also included a lot of session musicians and string sections, and that sort of thing.

But eventually they let the studio be used by external artists, who used the studio when Bronze artists weren't during the later 1970s.'

'The Roundhouse was opened in 1974, and, up until that time, studios had just been 16-track, and a couple that were just upgrading to 24, but Roundhouse had the purpose-built first 24-track studio and 24-track Studor tape machine. Some people thought it was a downgrade going to 24 tracks because we were still using two-inch tape, so you're putting 24 tracks on a tape as opposed to 16, so each track was getting less tape-width. So 16-track sounds better because the quality is better and signal-to-sound is better, but people wanted the tracks and were prepared to sacrifice a small amount of quality for the quantity of tracks because ultimately they were more important.'

'The console at the studio was purpose-built for the studio by Clive Green, who had a company called Cadac. Those boards were quite popular in the late 1970s and early 1980s. It was a massive L-shaped thing that had 24 outputs and 30 inputs, and had loads of switches and lots of relays which were always sticking. So you'd route something to a channel and think it was going there but it actually wasn't, and you'd sort of have to rattle the relay out of it before it would flick in.'

Engineer Dearnley recalled that, once the band had plugged in, 'We tracked the band live off the floor. In all the time I worked with AC/DC, that's always how we did it. I don't believe we used very many room mics in tracking that album, because the studio was just one big room with 40-foot-high ceilings, so the only way the guitars were separated was via baffles, so we had quite a bit of bleed in the room. Where that might have been a problem for other bands, it worked quite well for AC/DC because recording them is almost like recording a classical section – you take what they do, and perhaps edit between takes, but it's not recorded piece by piece like most other things at that time.'

Elaborating on this, drummer Phil Rudd explained to *Musician* magazine that what truly guided the band's studio synergy was 'a lot of human element in our music. It isn't perfect and it isn't meant to be. That can be a little frustrating when machines can nail everything. You can give people the wrong impression about your music when it is not in machine time. But the excitement is natural. There is a pregnant pause involved. When you play an accent, if you play it in a hurry it doesn't have any weight. You write the beat on the line in the music, but there is a lot of room around that line as to where it can actually go. The boys like that I don't play on top of things. They like it laid back, not on top. It is how you get excited about it. If you get in front of the beat, then all the weight is gone out of it. It gets light. You gotta maintain the weight ... I have never been a drummer's drummer. I am not a technical drummer. I don't make any claims to anything else.'

From an engineering perspective, Dearnley appreciated the band's approach to rocking and recording. Because of it, he remembered, 'they were very easy. I remember I was talking to Angus in Switzerland sometime after that album, and we were discussing record production, and Angus started tapping his foot on the floor and said, "Look, mate, if your fucking foot ain't tapping, it ain't the fucking master." Which is rule No. 1 of record production, especially with AC/DC. So they knew what they did and did it well.'

That said, the engineer did identify one trait that he felt made AC/DC unique. 'Most bands rotate around the feel of the drummer, whereas AC/DC rotates around Malcolm's feel, in my opinion. He's the one who absolutely sets it rock solid, and everyone sits down around him, and that's very unusual.'

Dearnley also recalled that working with the Young brothers was an exception to 'most groups I've worked with where there are siblings in bands, because they end up fighting a great deal, and you think blood's about to be spilled, and then the next moment they're absolutely fine again. I never saw any of that at all with AC/DC – everyone seems to get on and know their roles. So I never experienced a head-to-head with any of them.'

With the fundamentals established, the engineer said that producer Lange fitted perfectly into the fold because 'Mutt had a picture in his head of the way he wanted it to turn out, and he and I kept on working till you hit that picture — whether it was mic placement on the guitar amps or snare drum sounds. Mutt did a great deal of listening to what was going on — especially in America — and he very much did his homework about the way he wanted things to end up.'

Beginning with the album's drum sound, Dearnley explained that 'in those days, Roundhouse was set up very much as a classical studio, so we didn't have the amount of the dynamic mics we use now. So a lot of the mics we used would have been Neumanns, so I would have put a KM-84 on the snare/hi-hat, U-87s on the overheads, the AKG D202 that would have gone on the toms, the kick would have been an AKG D-12, and a U-47 would have been out in the room, maybe a foot away.

'That was an extension of something that had been drummed into my head very early on regarding the equilateral triangle of mic placement. That meant that wherever the sound was coming from, whether it's a violin or cello, the peak point is an equilateral triangle to the length of whatever's vibrating. So for a kick drum, if it was a 22-inch, it would have been 22 inches out, and then you adjusted to suit. That became more Mutt's domain, as he was very hands-on in the ideas department.'

One area Lange was squarely focused on was taking Bon Scott to new vocal heights in such a way that, according to the singer, 'the bottom line is still very much hard rock, but we've used more melody and backing vocals to enhance the sound. It's possible there is a more commercial structure to the music, without going the whole way. In the past, it's just been a total scream, so I worked on it a lot more this time.'

Despite the heavier emphasis placed on these enhancements, things went fine. Dearnley said that 'Bon would do a few takes, but I don't recall it being a painful process at all, just fine-tuning lyrics. For Bon, we used a Neumann U-67, and he would go stand in the studio and deliver.'

Capturing the Young brothers' raw power on to tape in a sound that *Kerrang!* would hail as the 'work of a cocksure, cock-waving band who know their time has come', Dearnley said, 'I remember using a couple of 57s and a 421 for Malcolm and Angus's amps each. Their cabinets would have been set up toward the corners, baffled off with half-baffles, and I was using close-mics – and juggling around with the cabinets to find the best speaker and the best position on that speaker.' When attention turned to overdubbing Angus's lead guitar solos, 'we'd lay everything off the floor, then later on replaced lead and backing vocals, and guitar solos with Angus sitting on the couch in the control room, using his radio pick-ups, cigarette hanging out of his mouth while he played. That was very much the way it was done every time.'

Delving into some of the inspiration behind what would become some of hard rock's most famous guitar solos, Angus revealed to *Guitar Player* that his secret was mainly being spontaneous. 'There are some things I've played where I've gone, "How in the hell did I do that?" You can sit there and try to figure it out for years, and there's nothing to match that. In the early days, if you were playing an A chord, you might play a solo that's in A. But then again, you might put progressions or notes in there that don't sound right. It sounds like you're playing in the wrong key or something, and sometimes that works ... But me, I can sit there and play it and I know how to get the sound of what I want.'

Listening from the console, Dearnley felt that Angus's 'guitar sounds are as much in the fingers as they are anywhere else. These guys absolutely have the techniques, and know exactly where to go.' Angus agreed, telling *Gibson* that it's the 'fingers more than anything. Sometimes I'll shake the neck a bit, because those necks get wobbly sometimes ... I've only got a small hand so I use all my fingers to bend. I really push it with all my fingers backing it up... [My speed comes] from my left hand. There's a lot I can do without picking.'

Detailing the inspiration behind the title track's signature riff – which the BBC would hail years later as an 'ever-green anthem', Malcolm told journalist Engleheart that 'there were hundreds of riffs going down every day, but this one we thought as we did it, "That's good, that one – we'll get back and listen to that." We kept moving on because we were on a bit of a roll and something else might come along. We got back to it the next day and it just stuck out like a dog's balls.'

In an interview with *Metal CD*, Malcolm praised both it and 'Touch Too Much', another of the LP's singles. '"Touch Too Much" was a hit off that record,' he recalled, '[but] the one song that stands out head and shoulders over everything else was the title track. If certain people had had their way, it wouldn't have been called "Highway to Hell" because the Bible Belt was very strong in America at the time and they made a fuss once the record came out. But, even though we were under pressure, we stuck to our guns.'

When attention turned to mixing, engineer Tony Platt took the reins from Mark Dearnley. 'This friend of mine I'd been running a studio for called me up one day and said, "A friend of mine is doing an album with this Australian punk band, and he wants somebody to mix it that knows that kind of Island rock sound, and I thought of you." So I spoke to Mutt, and went down to Roundhouse Studios, where they were starting to record *Highway to Hell*. Basically they only had enough budget to hire an external engineer for either the recording or the mix, and they decided to go with the mix. Mark Dearnley, who was the house engineer at Roundhouse at that time, recorded it, then Mutt and I took it over to Basing Street Studios to mix it. There were still some overdubs to finish off, like the vocal on "Night Prowler" and the backing vocals on "Highway to Hell" and a few guitar solos we finished off. On the little bit of vocal work I did with Mutt, I just stuck up an 87.'

Once he and Lange were into their task, Platt recalled that 'the challenge on mixing *Highway to Hell* was to glue it all together, because it had been recorded a bit separately. That's something Mutt's also always been very good at: making sure that the way the song is arranged is fitted together properly, so it actually went together quite quickly and easily.'

'I started off working with Mutt with a great deal of respect for him, and I think one of the things that used to work well with us was: Mutt was and still is something of a perfectionist. He had this sound in his head he wanted to go for, and he was able to explain that to me, and, once I got that in my head too, the two of us just went off and got it. He was using the reference points of where the sound is tight but you can still feel the space in between through the economy of faze.'

'Also the openness – there's something about a really good balance, and I think you can use the Rolling Stones as an example. When you listen to a mix of a Rolling Stones song, it feels like it could just fall apart at any moment – it's kind of hanging on by its fingertips – but is perfectly balanced, which adds an extra little bit of excitement to the mix as well. There's that little bit of ruggedness within the whole thing, and that I think was something we needed to achieve with AC/DC – not to polish it up too much. Make it listenable commercially, but not go too far with it.'

Describing the contrast between mixing at Basing Street

on a Helus console as opposed to Roundhouse's Cadac desk, Platt began by explaining that 'Roundhouse is a very dry, dense studio, so to deal with that I just employed a technique I'd used loads of times before and stuck a pair of Altec speakers up in the studio room, and used them as a chamber, and just fed bits and pieces through to kind of correct some ambient glue to glue it all together, and make things sound like they were a bit more in the same room. So that was one of the things that was necessary.'

'The beauty of mixing in those days was that there was precious little you had available to use for effects anyway, not that AC/DC let many effects go on their stuff. You had Echo Plate, the tape loop, you had compressors, and that was about it. We used just a little bit of slap echo and a little bit of reverb – very, very gingerly, because, with AC/DC, if they can hear it they don't like it. So you kind of use it just to push sounds forward, rather than using it as a halo effect.'

Detailing the fascinating process by which Lange mixed the rhythm section of Malcolm, Cliff Williams and Phil Rudd, Platt recalled that 'one of the things Mutt is particularly good at doing is making sure the instruments are tuned within the chord of the song, so that gives you a lot more possibilities. So, for instance, if you have a kick drum and the kick drum has a note in it, and the note that the kick drum has in it is not in the chord of the song, it's going to constantly be interfering with the sound of the bass. Or if you've got a snare drum that's got a note in it that is discordant with the guitar, then it's going to mess with the sound of the guitar. Whereas, if you tune it into the chord, and make sure the drums are ringing in tune with the rest, it just makes everything sound bigger and clearer.'

Angus told *Musician* magazine that, once the finished record had been handed in to a very happy Atlantic Records, the band felt equally satisfied about their debut collaboration with Lange. 'After we'd done the album, Bon said to Mutt, "I like what you've done. Do you think it would be worth it for me to go off and learn with somebody?" Mutt said, "No, I don't. This is you." And I think Mutt learned something from us as well. I think he was impressed that we could play and knew what a song was, as opposed to just a riff.'

On the album's release on 30 July 1979, the critics too were wowed by it, feeling it had broken a new kind of mainstream ground in hard rock. *Blender* magazine's later overview notes, 'Mutt Lange sanded off a few of AC/DC's rougher edges and bolted the steam-hammer riffs and Scott's foul wit to pop-friendly choruses.' The *Seattle Weekly* issued a challenge for the title track: 'Find me a better pure rock song (one not recorded by either AC/DC, Chuck Berry, or Jerry Lee Lewis), and I will buy you a beer!' And *Kerrang!* declared that the band 'sounds impossibly *ALIVE!*'

The album sold seven million copies and marked the band's US breakthrough into the Top 20 of the Billboard

Album Chart. Sadly, amid the astonishing success that would follow, life would soon change in a dark and irreversible way, threatening to end things for the band just as their reign over hard rock was beginning…

CHAPTER SIX

BACK IN BLACK (1980)

'Some bands fade when they try to adapt to what is
current. We play rock music. It's a little too late for us to
do a ballad. Rock is what we do best. Sometimes I'm
asked if I want to play music other than AC/DC. Sure, at
home I play a little blues, but after five minutes I'm like,
"Sod this!" and I'm playing hard rock again'

ANGUS YOUNG

'If *Highway to Hell* was the band's first major
blockbuster, *Back in Black* would prove rock's most
successful sequel in history.'

KERRANG!

Every rock fan owns a copy of *Back in Black*, whether on
vinyl, tape, CD or download. According to the BBC, the
album has sold 'an estimated 49 million units worldwide,
making it the highest-selling album by any band and the
second highest-selling album in history, behind *Thriller* by
Michael Jackson'. Despite this, as Reuters would report, 'in
1980 the Grammys showered statuettes on Christopher
Cross and Bob Seger' but years later the Grammy Academy
would celebrate the fact that, with the release of *Back in
Black*, the band had 'solidified themselves as Rock Gods'.

BACK IN BLACK (1980)

Pre-production had already begun on the album when a bolt from the blue hit the band. 'What happened was,' engineer Tony Platt recalled, 'Mutt and I were actually doing another album for another band called Mr Big – not the US band with Eric Martin but a UK band – and we were doing that at Battery Studios in London, going backwards and forwards with Malcolm and Angus, who were doing the pre-production and sending us tapes. Then one morning on those sessions, Mutt came in and said to me, "You're not going to believe this, but Bon's died."'

As Bon's official Australian fan site reported it, 'On 19 February 1980 … tragedy struck in London UK. Bon was found dead in a car after a night out. His official cause of death is acute alcoholic poisoning – death by misadventure. Bon was 33 years old when he passed away.'

Atlantic Records issued the following official press release after his sudden and shocking passing: 'Bon Scott was always the top joker in the AC/DC pack. The stories of his sexual and alcoholic excesses are legion and that part of his enormous fan mail that didn't involve tempting offers from young female fans invariably berated him for "leading poor Angus astray". Sadly, Bon is no longer with us after he tragically went just one step too far on one of his notorious boozing binges. But if there is a crumb of comfort to be found in such a needless and premature death, it is that Bon went out the way that he would have chosen, never flinching as he went over the top just one more time.'

Billboard would report years later that 'the grave site of AC/DC singer Bon Scott in Fremantle Cemetery in Western Australia was classified with a heritage listing … Even though heritage listings are usually reserved for buildings, the grave was recognised because of AC/DC's global popularity and because it is visited by thousands of fans each year.'

The band's first creative jam sessions for *Back in Black* – and sadly the Young brothers' last with Bon – were held between 12 and 15 February 1979 at E-Zee Hire Rehearsal Studio. 'Just a few days before he died,' Angus told *Brave Words/Bloody Knuckles*, 'he'd come down with me and Mal, he got behind the kit and Mal said to him, "Ah, Bon! Get on the drums, we need a drummer," and that's what he loved. Bon wanted to be the drummer in the band.'

'It was kind of funny – the first time we ever sat down, here's this guy saying, "I'm your new drummer." Mal convinced him to sing, to get up to the front of the stage. Then he was there at the end again. The last you saw him, there he was behind the kit. He played the intro to one of the tracks. It turned out it wasn't one of the greatest songs but the intro was great: "Let Me Put My Love Into You" – just the intro of it before it goes into Mutt Lange territory.'

Scott wanting to play the role of beat-keeper was part of the

Young brothers' pre-production routine before any album, Angus told rock journalist Murray Engleheart. '[It] was great for me and Mal because every now and again it would help, especially if we were writing songs. Because otherwise Malcolm would get behind the drum kit and I would do all the guitar work and/or bass, or Mal would get on the guitar and I'd try my hand at the kit.'

Even as the world reeled around them, the sudden loss of Bon Scott hit no one harder than the band. Malcolm – in an interview with *Classic Rock* – shared his memory of feeling a vast emptiness within the band. 'We were so depressed. We were just walking around in silence. Because there was nothing. Nothing.'

For Angus, the loss felt no different than if his own brother had died. 'For me it was like losing someone probably more than even in your family,' he revealed to rock journalist Paul Cashmere. 'We were very close as people. We were very, very tight. In a band like AC/DC it is like a childhood gang. We think the same. You spend so much time together that it is a very tough thing for you to go through.'

In addition to dealing with Scott's death on a personal level, the band had to face the elephant in the room on a professional one: the simple and obvious question of whether to continue on as a band or not. The question was answered, Angus recalled in an interview with *Gibson*, when 'Bon's father grabbed me and Malcolm and said, "Listen, you guys are young guys, so you've got to keep going." So that took a bit of pressure off us in a way because at the time we felt we didn't know which way it was going to go, because you might be seen as grave-robbing or something.'

Bon's mother Isa also approached the brothers at her son's funeral and gave them her blessing, telling the band, 'Go out there and find a new singer. You have to do it. Bon would have wanted it that way.'

Malcolm told *Mojo* that he felt the Scott family had 'accepted it more quickly than we had. When we were leaving, Bon's dad said, "You've got to find someone else, you know that," and we said, "We don't know what we're doing." He said, "Well, whatever you do don't stop."'

Even with the nod of Bon's parents, Malcolm remembered how, following the funeral, 'There was a nothingness around everyone – no ambition left, just nothing... When we got back to London the manager came up with a list of singers but I said, "I don't want to look at it." We still weren't interested. We thought, "We can't replace Bon – it's as simple as that." After a few weeks of sitting around and moping, I called Angus and said, "Do you want to go down to E-Zee Hire and maybe we can play around a bit?" So we just started playing together.'

Indeed, Angus credited Malcolm with motivating him to pick up his guitar again. 'It was my brother that picked me up a bit from his death,' he recalled to journalist Paul Stenning.

'He said to me, "Let's get together and just continue what we were doing." We were writing songs at the time Bon died. He said, "Let's continue doing that." It kept you going and was good therapy, I suppose.' Besides, as Angus would quip to *Juke* magazine, 'Bon would have kicked us all up the arse if we'd split!'

AC/DC's decision to treat the studio as their therapy following Bon's death was possibly the best path the band could have followed to get themselves, and their fans, going again. As Angus told *Classic Rock*, 'I guess we retreated into our music. At the time, we weren't thinking very clearly. But we decided working was better than sitting there, still in shock about Bon. So in some ways it was therapeutic, you know.'

Malcolm added in a frank conversation with *Brave Words / Bloody Knuckles* that the band's decision to regroup 'made us grow up really quickly I think … We just got a hold of each other one day and just said, "Look, we've come up with lots of music before Bon died, so why don't we just get together and sit down and at least … at least we can do something, we can play guitar." So we did that and a lot of good music came from that period because something kicked in there. We didn't have to do it, but inside there was stuff coming out that probably wouldn't have ever appeared.'

Once the brothers got back to work on new demos for what they'd already decided would be their tribute to Bon,

Angus recalled that it was still a struggle to get past the fact that 'Malcolm and I were really looking forward to getting him into the studio and doing the next album more than we've done with any album before. Because, after the success of the last one, it was going to be a really big challenge. That was the sad part of it all because perhaps it could have been the best thing he'd ever done on record. That would have been the crowning glory of his life.'

But how to replace him? Malcolm told journalist Engleheart, 'Me and Angus had been together two weeks jamming and after [Bon's death] and we thought, "Well, this is it really. I just can't see David Coverdale singing with the band, you know what I mean?" Nothing looked appealing out there. There was no incentive, we were all quite shocked about it. But after a couple weeks of sitting around, we had to do something – you're sitting at home all the time doing nothing. So we decided to get back to these couple of riffs that we'd put together and we just carried on through that. But because Bon wasn't there, it gave us so much more determination. We had to do something – you know, you had to get your energies out…'

'It was a real gut-wrenching thing, the whole episode, and we didn't still know what was going to happen. You were sort of in a limbo world and I think that came through in all the stuff we came up with on that record. We always thought that Bon was with us in that too, you know what I mean? He was a big part of what we were doing, and his spirit was all over it because the energy was coming from Bon.'

Feeling bleak about the various alternatives that their management suggested as potential replacements for Bon – including Gary Holton of the Heavy Metal Kids – the band decided to audition for a new singer. 'After a while,' Angus recalled in an interview with *Classic Rock*, 'when we felt we were close to having all the songs together, we knew we had to confront the question of a new singer. But it wasn't like we put an advertisement in a music paper that said: "AC/DC wants a new front man." No… that would have been too over the top. It was subtler than that. People like Bon are unique. They're special. And we didn't want someone to come in and copy him. If anything, we wanted someone who was his own character.'

Engineer Tony Platt described an environment where 'everything was kind of up in the air for a little while, then the band decided they were just gonna go ahead. So, while Mutt and I were still wrapping up the Mr Big album, AC/DC started auditioning for new singers. So, instead of getting pre-production tapes every morning, we were getting audition tapes with different singers [and] giving the band feedback: "Well, he sounds kind of good, he doesn't sound so great, that one's a definite no." For me, it was a little bit confusing because I was trying to pay attention to the album we were doing, so we'd listen on Mutt's car stereo on the way into the studio, make our notes, and then get on with the other session.'

Among those who came very close was Allen Fryer, the son of another Scottish family who had emigrated to Australia, and who had the support of Harry Vanda and George Young. (Fryer would end up in a band called Heaven.) But the magic moment for everyone came the day Geordie singer Brian Johnson's name was thrown in the hat. And, in fact, it was Bon Scott who had first tipped the band off about the singer.

'I remember the first time I had ever heard Brian's name was from Bon,' Angus told *Brave Words/Bloody Knuckles*. 'Bon had mentioned that he had been in England once touring with a band, and that Brian had been in a band called Geordie. And Bon had said, "Brian Johnson – he was a great rock 'n' roll singer in the style of Little Richard." And that was Bon's big idol, Little Richard. I think, when he saw Brian at that time, to Bon it was, "Well, he's a guy that knows what rock 'n' roll is all about."'

In an interview with the *Guardian*, Angus added, '[Bon said] about that night, "There's this guy up there screaming at the top of his lungs and then the next thing you know, he's hit the deck. He's on the floor, rolling around and screaming. I thought it was great, and then to top it off – you couldn't get a better encore – they came in and wheeled the guy off!"'

But the reality was painfully different, as Johnson confirmed in an interview with *Reader's Digest*. 'I was in a little band called Geordie and we were in this horrible place up north on a horrible cold night and I had appendicitis. He [Bon] was watching with his then band, Fraternity. I was in agony – I got carried out.'

Bon's story about Johnson's passion as a performer and vocalist intrigued Angus. 'We wanted someone who could do what Bon did and was a real character,' he told *Juke* magazine, 'but we didn't want someone who was just a perfect imitation of him.' The seed had been sown, as he recalled to rock journalist Paul Stenning. 'Brian's name came up right away… At the time I said, "Maybe check out this guy Brian and see what he's doing."'

As Johnson told *Mojo*, everything seemed to happen very fast. 'Malcolm phoned me up on Grand National Day 1980 and said, would I like to come and have a shot with the boys? I was a huge fan of Bon Scott's – still am, I still play his records – a real sleazy voice, the sneakiest voice ever for blues.'

When Johnson showed up for his audition, Malcolm – in an interview with *Mojo* – shared the touching memory that 'he had tears in his eyes – he was as sad about Bon as we were. Anyway, we said, "Do you want to give it a go?" And he said, "I do 'Whole Lotta Rosie' with Geordie," and off he went. We went, fucking hell, this guy is cutting the mustard. "Anything else you know?" "Nutbush City Limits?" "OK, we can knock that out," and he sang that great too. It put a little smile on our faces – for the first time since Bon.'

Johnson felt equally fortunate to have found the band, recalling in an interview with Triple M Radio Australia that 'my band Geordie had a few hits and I left with less money than when I'd joined. I swore I'd never get bitten by the rock 'n' roll bug again... But I was 32 when I met Mal and Angus. I thought, "What harm can it do to sing a few songs with them?" When I did, I got goosebumps like I'd never had before. These guys shook the shit out of me. I thought I'd give it another shot. I'm pleased I did.'

Landing the gig with one of the biggest bands in hard rock was 'a bit of fucking luck, really,' he told Engleheart. 'Everybody gets a break in life, I suppose – you've got to get ahold of it with both hands and use it.'

Seeking a change of pace to suit a fresh start with a new singer, the band opted to retreat from the headlines and heartaches in London and take up recording residence in the Bahamas, specifically the island of Nassau and the legendary Compass Point Studios, which had been built by Island Records founder Chris Blackwell.

According to the studio's publicity, Compass Point offers artists the opportunity to create in an environment where they first 'rise in the morning for a swim in the warm tropical waters. Stroll or jog along a beautiful beach. Enjoy a gourmet breakfast under a palm-covered veranda. Then make the short walk to one of the world's most famous, spacious and well-equipped studios to begin your day's work. Any time you need a break, just step outside and gaze across an endless seascape of ocean blue, breathe in the fresh sea air, and then come back refreshed. When the day's work is finished, leisurely stroll home under a canopy of brilliant stars. Compass Point Studios in Nassau, Bahamas, have been the "Home Studio to the Stars" now for 33 years. The history of what has been recorded here is virtually unmatched in the industry.'

In the late '70s and mid-'80s, Compass Point was one of the great recording studios of the world. 'Artists came from around the world to record in the Bahamas,' the studio adds. 'Many major producers utilised the facilities, including Chris Blackwell himself, in his role as record producer. The resulting records sold in the many millions of copies worldwide. AC/DC's *Back in Black*, widely regarded as the ultimate, and largest selling rock album of all time, was just one of the many great albums recorded at Compass Point Studios.'

Other well-known artists who used Compass Point in its early days were the Rolling Stones, U2, Robert Palmer, The B-52's, Talking Heads, Dire Straits, Bob Marley, Eric Clapton, The Cure, David Bowie, Judas Priest, Iron Maiden, Mick Jagger, Whitesnake, ELO, Status Quo, Tom Tom Club, Joe Cocker, Emerson Lake and Palmer, Eurythmics, Power Station, Roxy Music, Bad Company and many others.

According to Blackwell, 'I decided to build a studio in a restful location ... and I built it from scratch. A man who worked at the studio at Island's offices in London was the sound designer and he created a magic room.'

Elaborating on the technical side, journalist David Katz explained that Blackwell had 'conceived of Compass Point as a giant blank canvas for audio, a space where music could be made without the distraction of external influence ... Construction of the 24-track facility took place in 1977, with an MCI 500 series mixing desk and other top-notch equipment installed, initially in one room. High-profile recording sessions took place almost from its very inception: in March and April 1978, Talking Heads made the first of many appearances there to record *More Songs About Buildings and Food*. 1979 began with Dire Straits' second album, *Communique*, and immediately after, the Rolling Stones were in residence for a month to work on *Tattoo You*.

'In fact, so many mainstream rock acts were booking the place that Blackwell had to build Studio B, a second recording room, to ensure enough time was available for his own projects. It was towards the end of 1979 that Compass Point really came into its stride.'

Angus, for the band's part, told Stenning, 'There were a lot of different reasons for us finally deciding to work out there. Tax was one of them, and another was the actual availability of studios. We wanted somewhere in England because the country has a great working atmosphere. We didn't really want to go over to Europe since most of the stuff from there tends to be disco. There was one in Sweden that Led Zeppelin used, but that belongs to ABBA, and at that point they themselves were using it. But we didn't want to hang around waiting, we just wanted to get on with it.'

Malcolm added in a conversation with *Classic Rock* that for the band at that time 'it was the best place to do that album because there was nothing going on. We'd sit through the night with a couple of bottles of rum with coconut milk and work. That's where a lot of the lyrical ideas came from.'

As idyllic as the Bahamas might sound as a recording backdrop, Brian Johnson told rock journalist Susan Masino that the reality was rather different. 'It wasn't a tropical paradise. It wasn't all white beaches,' he said. 'It was pissing down, there was flooding, and all the electricity went out – nae television!'

There were other problems, too, as Angus told the BBC. 'At the time they were having problems. A few tourists had been killed on the beach and then we got robbed. We were all out there in these little huts … And the lady who used to come round who looked after the place, she had a big machete. She used to say, "Listen, if anyone sticks their head through that door and you don't know them, chop it off!"'

Malcolm joked that 'you ended up having to guard your stuff with spears', but he also admitted to the BBC that indeed 'it was quite scary sometimes, and at the same time losing Bon and all… It was a hard album to make.'

AC/DC IN THE STUDIO

Having got started on recording, engineer Tony Platt described, 'After *Highway to Hell* there were certain things I wanted to achieve when I was asked to go and do *Back in Black*. I wanted to start out with more ambience on the drums, and wanted there to be more leakage between the guitars and the drums. We recorded *Back in Black* much more live I think than *Highway to Hell* was recorded, and I wanted to employ those techniques of allowing controlled leakage between the instruments.'

'So when we got to Compass Point – which was sort of a strange place to go off and do a rock record – I might have perhaps, had I been given the choice, chosen a studio with a higher ceiling and a larger floor area. But we were in that studio for reasons that were not necessarily creative, so I had to work out what I was going to do with this room to achieve those aforementioned sonic goals.'

'So what I did was walk around the room with a snare drum, hitting it, to see if there was a part of the room that was going to sound better than another part of the room. And there was this one particular spot right in the middle of the room, where the snare drum sounded bigger and brighter and louder than it did anywhere else, and it turned out the ceiling was a little higher at that point. So we set the drum kit up with the snare right underneath that, and the kick drum just a little bit in front, and, just by using natural acoustics, we managed to create a way of controlling the way the sound of the drums leaked on to everybody else.'

Once the drum kit was set up, Platt described his miking technique. 'I would have miked the kick drum either with a D-20 or a U-47 Phet, the tom toms would have been RE-20s or SM-7s, and the snare most certainly was a KM-86 on the top, and an SM-57 underneath. The under-snare mic, the SM-57, is a very robust microphone and you don't need a lot of fidelity from that. I like to use a condenser on top because I want to get the sound of the whole drum – I don't want a narrow dynamic sound field on the top of the snare drum. Phil's not necessarily a heavy hitter, he's just a good hitter. In actual fact, it was the same with John Bonham – he didn't necessarily hit the drums really hard. Quite often, I've found with drummers that do hit very, very hard, they don't sound nearly as loud, because they're deadening the sound of the drum by hitting it so hard. I prefer to try and come up with a way of controlling the hi-hat on the leakage, and have a big sounding snare.'

Warming to his subject, he added, 'Some of the things I brought to the engineering on those AC/DC records were techniques that I was always working with and developing in any case. One of the things I picked up from Mutt – I used to do it automatically but I became a little bit more fixated on doing it – was getting the tom toms to be tuned within the chord in the key of the song. So that, again, when you're putting all these frequencies together, what you don't want is to have them fighting with each other. So it means the tom toms can occupy a space within the whole sound that is there for them. So, if every time the floor tom gets hit, you get dissonance between the note on the floor tom and one of the notes on the bass, it actually takes up rather a lot of space in the mix. You lose a lot of clarity, and therefore you lose a lot of punch and a lot of power.'

In crafting their sonic goals for *Back in Black*, the band deferred in part to producer Mutt Lange. Angus – in an interview with *Classic Rock* – described feeling a sense of relief that the producer was willing to stick by the band's side. 'It was very good for both us and him I think. After he made *Highway to Hell* he was in big demand, but I thought it was good for him [to work with us again]. Especially after what happened to us. It's to Mutt's credit that he still wanted to be involved with us after Bon's death.'

Engineer Tony Platt explained that, heading into tracking, 'there was very much a consensus on *Back in Black* actually between Mutt and the band, in part because I think Mutt – at that point in time – had not become completely a perfectionist, so he was still able to stand back from that a little bit, and the band remained very much a part of the decision-making process throughout. So, when we were tracking, we'd do several takes, and some of the songs were edited from more than one take, but Mutt and the band would all sign off together.'

It was through this creative collaboration, Malcolm told *Mojo*, that a healing process began, such that 'we became a very close, tight unit'.

Recording in Compass Point's Studio A, which Platt recalled had an MCI console and MCI tape machine, they paid primary attention to tracking guitars, creating a sound that the BBC would hail as 'heavy-riffed and big-hearted'. Platt said that 'the combination between Malcolm and Angus's guitars was important too, so, as they were playing, Mutt and I were trying to blend the sound in a way that captured the song the best of all. It wasn't so much what I did right in that, but what I didn't do wrong, because, when these guys are playing, they play rock music better than anyone else, period – better than any other band on the planet as far as I'm concerned. So really what I had to do was not fuck it up. I know that sounds very simplistic, but, when you've got people like that, it does make you sound good naturally.

'It's very, very straightforward. There were no double-tracked guitars on those AC/DC albums. There's one track of Malcolm, one track of Angus, and then Angus would continue to play rhythm after he finished his solos so you didn't get a drop in dynamics. So the only time that there was a third guitar playing rhythm was after the solos.'

Feeling that the heart of AC/DC's driving guitar sound stemmed from the brothers' innate musical ties, the engineer explained, 'Angus isn't the greatest rhythm guitarist in some respects, whereas Malcolm's probably one of the best rhythm guitar players known to man. So what makes them play so magically together is: they have a very simple technique where they basically play in unison but they play in different positions, playing different inversions of the same chords. So you don't get that kind of chorusy effect from the two guitars playing in unison that you would get if they were playing in the same position – it just sounds like one big guitar.'

Angus described to *Guitar Player* how the brothers' guitar-layering process was an organic one. '[Double-tracking has] never been an important element. I'd rather go for something that's natural than double-track. You can make it sound thick by double-tracking. You can make it sound quiet; you can add acoustic guitars to bring it down. There are a lot of tricks like that. We've done things in the past, but it's mainly been the natural sound that we've always ended up with... The hard rhythm is how Malcolm plays, and between him, Phil and Cliff, they hold down that back line rhythm, and it allows Brian and I to be the colour.'

When Platt and Lange were working individually with Angus on his solo overdubs, the engineer recalled, 'Angus was fairly quick recording his solos. We'd do maybe two or three, do a little comp between them, or drop-ins if necessary, stuff like that, but both he and his brother are very instinctive players. They don't overthink things — they just get on and do it. It's just a good bit of solid Scottish-Australian attitude.'

Of the technical set-up to capture the guitar sound, Platt explained, 'We built booths for the guitars where we could have them open or closed, and open them up to any degree we wanted to, so I could then control the amount of leakage that was going out into the room. I didn't use any compressors at all on the guitars.

'To record the guitars, we were using amp heads and 4x12s, so quite often the amp head would be outside the booth, and the 4x12 would be inside the booth, but we had lots of combinations — 50 watt heads, 100 watt heads, and different 4x12 cabinets. Over a period of time, you learn which ones do which job best, so I was always choosing the combinations I thought worked best. My preference on guitar miking is to use U-67s and U-87s, and I used two of them, which is based off something that occurred to me a long, long time ago. To get a sound to spread across the stereo, if you've got it recorded in stereo with two microphones, then you can actually spread the sound and don't have to have it quite as loud.'

Angus added in an interview with *Guitar Player*, 'Most people hear distortion [on our records] … and they think it's loud. We keep it as clean as possible. The cleaner you do it, the louder it will sound when they do the cutting of it.'

Turning to Cliff Williams's bass tracking, Platt added, 'There was a DI on the bass, and two microphones, a D-20 and a 47 Phet. I picked up my preference for using two mics on a bass from previous demos I'd recorded with Thin Lizzy. Phil Lynott used to have two stacks – an acoustic 361 and a Hi-Watt 4x12 stack – and a Rickenbacker stereo bass that actually had been wired so the same signal came out of both sides. He used to put stuff through the acoustic 361 so he could get the bottom end, and the Hi-Watt to get the overdriven top end. So you have to mic that up with two microphones, which led me to thinking, "Well, this is cool actually. Instead of trying to get lots of bottom out of one microphone and top out of the same one, why don't I have a microphone I can get lots of nice bottom out of, and another I can get lots of top out of, and put the two mics together? Then I won't have to EQ things nearly as much." So it became one of those practical techniques that I've taken with me, and one I used on *Back in Black*.'

Of the specific inspiration behind the title track's legendary riff – one that the *Guardian* would point out years later 'remains a bedroom guitarist's rite-of-passage, still pertinent in the Guitar Hero age' – Angus revealed to *GuitarWorld* that it almost didn't come about. 'During the *Highway to Hell* tour,' he recalled, 'Malcolm came in one day and played me a couple of ideas he had knocked down on cassette, and one of them was the main riff for "Back in Black". And he said, "Look, I've got this riff and it's driving me nuts ... it's been bugging me, this track. What do you think?"

'It's three in the morning and I'm trying to sleep, and he's saying, "What do you think of this?" I said, "Sounds fine to me" ... He was going to wipe it off and reuse the tape, because cassettes were a hard item for us to come by sometimes! I said, "Don't trash it. If you don't want it, I'll have it" ... In fact, I was never able to do it exactly the way he had it on tape. To my ears, I still don't play the thing right!'

Stepping up to the mic – and to the plate in filling some very large shoes – Brian Johnson candidly admitted to *Mojo*, 'I was scared shitless ... but they never made me feel like I was standing in a dead man's shoes.' He added to journalist Stenning that he remembered standing at the mic 'thinking, "Is this gonna work out right? If it doesn't work out right, I'm gonna be the biggest scapegoat the world's ever known." If it didn't work out well, they could have just said, "That's a waste of time," thrown it in the bin and said, "Let's try it with someone else." That was all running through my mind because I didn't realise what I had taken on.'

To Johnson's relief, all went well. Angus told rock journalist Susan Masino 'he more or less fitted in straight away', with Malcolm chipping in, 'Brian sang great. It put a little smile on our face ... for the first time since Bon.'

As he sat behind the console tracking Johnson's vocals day in and out, Tony Platt said, 'You had to take your hat off to him. For somebody to walk into that situation under those circumstances and perform like that, it's an incredible thing.

'You also have to remember it's actually quite difficult in a climate like the Bahamas, because it's an air-conditioned environment. And because you can't turn the air conditioning off, you've just got pure oxygen, so at times it was too humid, at times it was too dry. And we had to be very careful with Brian coming in and out of the studio, down the corridor and into the control room, because he'd come out of an air-conditioned environment, into a hot corridor, then back into an air-conditioned environment, and that's just asking for trouble. So we had to be very considerate to him, and a lot of the time he just stayed in the studio room, and we just played stuff back down the headphones to him.

'Angus and Malcolm would wander off and come back in to check on how vocals were going, but it was primarily Brian, Mutt and I. Vocally, we used a U-67 and a U-87, depending on the song. The thing about Brian's voice is it projects really well. Still, it was tough at times tracking his vocals because some of those notes are pretty damn high, and he had to work very, very hard.'

In addition to the pressure of living up to the band's expectations, Brian faced the added stress of living up to those of producer Mutt Lange. 'I gained such an incredible respect for him,' Platt said of the singer. 'That was the point at which Mutt was absolutely a stickler for getting every single note and every single syllable as good as it possibly could be, and it's one of the features of the album. A lot of people focus on the drums and guitars, but, let's face it, those vocals absolutely finish it off, top it off to the most incredible extent.'

To Johnson and the producers' relief, the team had pulled off the kind of success that no one had expected. As Johnson revealed to Paul Stenning, 'I was so relieved at the end, when the first phone call came through from the manager saying, "Oh great, brilliant." And Atlantic phoned up and said, "Fantastic, it's gonna do the business." For three days when I came back from the Bahamas, I just sat in the chair at home and didn't move.'

Tour manager Ian Jeffery recalled to Engleheart that the band had had the opposite reaction once Brian had laid his vocals. After one particularly blazing playback, he said, 'You could feel the hairs on the back of your neck stand up. Angus gets out of his seat from his cross-legged position and his right leg's on the go. We're off and racing!'

Atlantic Records president Phil Carson was equally excited, adding, 'Brian is a brilliant front man.'

Prior to departing for the States, Johnson told journalist Masino that one of his proudest moments in the course of recording the album had come when he laid the vocals for the title track 'Back in Black'. In an interview with *Classic Rock*, he conjured up a scene where 'it was about three in the afternoon, it was a beautiful sunny day, and I went outside down to where the huts were. I sat on this wall and I got a ciggie out and sat among the trees. I was so happy that I had done it. But I hadn't really heard the song. I'd go in and do a couple of verses, pop back and do a chorus. That's the way Mutt keeps you interested, you know.'

Malcolm revealed in an interview with Stenning that 'we got the title for the album before we'd even written a tune. Angus said, "Why not call it *Back in Black*, make a black album cover and then it's for Bon."'

Angus confirmed this to *Melody Maker*. 'We all decided that it was a far better tribute to call the whole thing *Back in Black* – that way the album is dedicated to him rather than just one little line in the back of the sleeve. It goes a lot deeper than that.'

Angus also revealed in an interview with Engleheart that, as production neared completion, he even went up against producer Lange on the question of the album's title. 'Mutt asked me what we were going to call this record. I said, "*Back in Black*," and he said, "You don't think that's morbid?" I said, "No, because it's for Bon – it's our tribute to him and that's what it's going to be!" And he was a bit taken aback. I said to him, "Mutt, listen – when we did *Highway to Hell*, you were freaking out. You were saying, 'Radio won't play it, and the Midwest, they're very religious, they won't play this record.'" And I said, "Mutt, they were the first people to play it." I said, "The only thing I know is we go out there and play in front of people, so at least allow us that factor. This is what we were built for, to go on stage. This is what we do best. At least allow us the courtesy of trusting our judgement on this."'

The fact that the band had written the title track and broader album as a tribute to Bon Scott was a process Johnson had come fully prepared to respect, but instead found the band welcomed him into that creative nerve-centre, and he told Stenning that 'they never made me feel left out'. So inclusive was the atmosphere that the singer admitted he got butterflies once they asked him to contribute to the writing of the title track. In an interview with Heather Mills, Johnson recalled that, though he was nervous, once the Young brothers had asked, there was no way out. 'The guys just said, "Would you try?" And luckily enough I came up with some useful lyrics. The lads had all the titles ready for us. "Back in Black" was particularly difficult because the boys were saying, "We want this song in memory of [Bon]..." It was pretty tough, but I think we managed it pretty good, you know?'

Certainly, the *Guardian* was impressed, saying its 'sky-scraping verse, with its themes of immortality, was a typically audacious way for the band to reaffirm itself'.

In his other lyric writing for the album, Brian told Stenning that the difference between his and Bon's writing style was that 'Bon's songs were more like documentaries. They were very true to life. Mine were just instances in life put together.'

In the course of crafting 'You Shook Me All Night Long' – which *Billboard* would call 'the greatest one-night-stand anthem in rock history' – Brian drew on his tropical surroundings for inspiration. Brian confessed to Stenning that when he wrote 'the line "Knockin' me out with those American thighs" – I hadn't been even in America at the time. But we were in the Bahamas and I had seen a couple of American girls, and they were just so beautiful. They were blond, bronzed and tall... I'd never seen anyone that beautiful before. So I was just using my imagination, what I would do if I could. Bon had done it all.'

Clearly, Johnson held a deep respect for Scott's legacy and talent. 'I think Bon Scott had a bit of genius,' he told the BBC. 'It annoys me that nobody has recognised that before. He used to sing great words, write great words. He had a little twist in everything he said. Nobody ever recognised the man at the time. Oh great, when the man died they were starting to say, "Yeah, the man was a genius." That was too late; it's not fair. I think he was so clever, and I think he had such a distinct voice as well. He was brilliant.'

Producer Mutt Lange pushed AC/DC hard in the studio towards achieving their absolute best sonically and in terms of songwriting. Engineer Mike Shipley, who would go on to work with Lange on the Def Leppard albums *Pyromania* and *Hysteria* – explained of Lange's processes to *Mix Online* that, even though extremely methodical, he was never out of control. 'With Mutt, because he's so involved in the whole process, he'd get to a stage where you had a song finished, we thought. We'd busted our balls, spending days on guitar sounds, days on vocal sounds – and he'd change the chorus. But see, there's no sense having an attitude or ever thinking for even a second that having an attitude is going to do anything but make the process really hard for anybody else. All having an attitude will do is get in the way of what the rest of the process is supposed to be, which is people like Mutt and whoever is in the band getting what they want.'

What Lange wanted, ultimately, was a moment where 'sometimes when you're lucky in life you can make the trends happen. It's always by accident and chance, but it happens ... It's difficult to create music that people will listen to over and over again.'

Once team AC/DC had wrapped production on *Back in Black*, they relocated from the tropical backdrop of the Bahamas to the urban one of New York City to mix the album. The magnitude – both personally and musically – of what the band had pulled off in regrouping and recording their tribute to Bon just months after his passing – didn't immediately dawn on them. Malcolm told *Mojo* that he didn't gain perspective on this surreal time 'until we got out of the Bahamas and into the mixing room in New York. After about a week of not hearing any of it we thought, "Fucking hell, this is a monster!" And sure enough, it was.'

Back in Black was to be mixed in Studio A at Electric Ladyland, the studio founded by the late guitar god Jimi Hendrix. Describing the equipment, its website says of the console in Studio A: 'Designed in 1972, the Neve 1081 was originally conceived as a combined mic/line preamp and equaliser section for the Neve modular consoles. A glance through the credits on today's platinum-selling albums reveals that these vintage consoles are still widely used to great effect, confirming the 1081's status as a truly classic component in a recording front-end or mixing environment. Hand-built 1081 modules are still crafted in Burnley, UK much the same way as the original modules, using the original components, hand-wound transformers and time-honed construction methods. Electric Ladyland's Studio A offers 16 of these vintage mic pre's, which three decades of studio engineering have considered indispensable for recording and mixing drums, bass percussion.'

Engineer Tony Platt recalled, 'Electric Ladyland in New York was a great place to mix. We still had overdubbing to do, some backing vocals, and some bits and pieces to finish up.'

Setting his ears to the task of mixing *Back in Black* was producer Mutt Lange – who *Time* magazine would hail a 'genius' in connection with the album's 'sonic quality' and 'arena anthems of uncorrupted hookiness'.

In a reflection of just how focused Lange liked to be the moment he sat down behind the mixing board, Platt offered a humorous memory from that preparatory process. 'Working with Mutt I had gotten into the habit of going into the studio the day before and checking the monitors so I knew they were all working. So I went into Electric Lady the day before, and they had this Quad-Amped Westlake system in that room. So I started listening to the tapes in there, and was absolutely certain there was something wrong on one side because I switched the snare from one side to the other and it didn't sound right. And the tech at the time – Sal, who went on to build Paisley Park for Prince – was fantastic, because he said, "Well, I can't hear what you're hearing, but, if you say you're hearing it, I believe you," and off he went to find out what it was.

'He ended up stripping both of the monitors down, and found that there was a cracked diaphragm in the mid-unit of one side of the monitors. Funnily enough, it was on the side that I thought sounded OK. That was a big lesson to me, because I was listening to the snare coming through, and wasn't listening to the way I knew it was, I was listening to the way I thought it might sound good. And of course, the cracked diaphragm on the mid-driver was giving it a little extra ring, which I was liking, but in fact it was the monitor was wrong.'

'So we put all that back together, and then we voiced the room. It was the one and only time that Mutt walked in the room and listened to the monitors, and said, "Yeah, they sound good." Normally, he was never satisfied with the monitoring in the room. So we started out from a very, very good place in that respect.'

Heading into the process, Lange and Platt began with the album's drums, with the engineer recalling that 'it was a pretty dry mix. There is a little bit of a slap and a little bit of reverb, and I did have ambience microphones – 87s – I'd recorded, so I was able to use a natural room sound. I like 87s for their natural sound – 87s are not great bottom-end microphones, but the top end is always very clear and detailed. You get plenty of detail off them, and they're great workhorse microphones.'

In more general terms, Platt added, 'With Mutt, I would spend a bit of time getting the sounds sorted out in the right places, and then the thing we paid most attention to while mixing was getting the blend and the balance right. We mostly achieved that by turning everything down and mixing in mono through an Oratone. Once you know the sounds are the sounds that you want, there's no real point in just impressing yourself every time you play back – what you really want to do is hear how the instruments relate to each other. So you turn the song right down, especially if you put it into mono, and you can hear the inter-relationship between the instruments, and make sure you get that balance so no one's covering anyone else up – you can hear everything clearly. What happens when you turn that up is it just gets bigger and bigger and bigger the louder you turn it.'

Homing in on one of the dynamics that made *Back in Black* such a brilliant pop/hard-rock album, Platt said, 'One of the reasons Mutt was so successful was he had an ear for what was going to be good on the radio. That brings up a funny story actually, because, when we were finished mixing, Mutt and I ended up having to present the album to a room full of marketing people from Atlantic at Rockefeller Plaza. I wanted to make sure it was absolutely spot-on, so I made a special copy of it on quarter-inch tape, took a Revox in and a really good hi-fi system. So we played it in this boardroom fairly loud, and this assembled gathering of marketing people sat around, didn't really look too wowed at first. That put it into a real perspective for me. We weren't there to speak up for the song, just to play it.'

In the end, 'You Shook Me All Night Long' spoke for itself, becoming a favourite Friday-night anthem, whether at a high-school dance, a singles bar or in the back of a car. For Platt, perhaps the greatest sonic accomplishment he and producer Mutt Lange achieved came with that song and the broader album. 'One of the things I think we started to achieve on *Highway to Hell*, and that we definitely achieved on *Back in Black* is it's a record that still sounds as ballsy if you play it quiet as if you play it loud. And I've heard it on systems all over the world. I think my biggest buzz ever was walking into Madison Square Garden before a Van Halen concert as they were doing the soundcheck. I walked into the arena literally as the sound guy was putting *Back in Black* on, and the hairs went up on the back of my neck hearing that played over such a big system. The clarity of it was still there, that was the thing. It wasn't just loud, it was loud and clear.'

Equally loud and clear were the bells tolling for the band's dearly departed brother and singer Bon Scott at the top of the album. It was a tribute that Angus told rock journalist Ethan Schlesinger he liked 'because it makes a brilliant sound and it was fitting for the time we went through after Bon's death and *Back in Black*'.

On a lighter note, Angus also quipped to journalist Paul Stenning that the departed singer's spirit still showed up in the band's newest music, 'sometimes when we're recording, I do a double take because I can feel something, that Bon edge. Hopefully he's still plugging in and hearing what we're about.'

With the spirit of Bon Scott at their back, the band produced a truly inspired accomplishment in the completion of *Back in Black*. Although Bon had only passed away in February, the band had the LP wrapped and in the stores by July of the same year. Following its release on 25 July 1980, *Back in Black* hit the

Billboard Top 200 Album Chart at No. 4 and, like its predecessor *Highway to Hell*, would remain on the charts for more than a year and a half as the world at large fell instantly in love with AC/DC's revitalised line-up.

'If *Highway to Hell* was the band's first major blockbuster,' *Kerrang!* declared, '*Back in Black* would prove rock's most successful sequel in history.' Elsewhere, *Time* counted *Back in Black* as one of its Top 100 Best Albums of All Time, and *Gentleman's Quarterly Australia* crowned the album No. 1 on their list of the Top 50 Most Influential Australian Albums. Even the BBC hailed *Back in Black* – 30 years after its release – as a classic that 'just does not get old'.

There was a warm reception, too, for Brian Johnson's courageous efforts. The *LA Times* noted, 'Brian Johnson was miraculously able to do what Scott had done before,' while *Time* magazine celebrated the fact that 'Brian Johnson, in his rookie campaign replacing the late Bon Scott, sings as if he's being tortured – and thoroughly enjoying it!'

For the band, the greatest accolade they could receive was from their die-hard fan base embracing a band that Angus told Engleheart he had felt only a few months earlier 'was the end, to be honest'. In a conversation with interviewer Paul Cashmere, he added, 'It was a big decision whether we would go on or stop ... I think the hardest thing was to decide, but ever since then we have only ever gone forward ... with a positive attitude.'

AC/DC IN THE STUDIO

According to *Kerrang!* the consequences of the band's decision to press on turned 'AC/DC into the biggest band in the world and influenced literally thousands of young musicians'.

As lead vocalist Brian Johnson recalled of the whirlwind that followed the release of *Back in Black*, 'that was obviously the golden era but I was too busy to enjoy it or remember it. When I came back I was at home for two weeks sitting there going, "Did that really happen? Nah…" and suddenly it was America, stadiums, a flurry of work. We never stopped.' Indeed, less than a year later the band headed straight back into the studio to begin work on the follow-up – for which they were to be saluted.

CHAPTER SEVEN

FOR THOSE ABOUT TO ROCK (WE SALUTE YOU) (1981)

'Middle-aged critics hate them, moms and
dads blanch, the kids cheer on. AC/DC is the latest
musical weapon in the war between the generations.
Some say they're faceless – but try to convince
your 13-year-old cousin'
NEWSWEEK, 1982

Following up what was either the first or second greatest hard-rock album of all time – depending on whether you rank *Highway to Hell* ahead of *Back in Black* or vice versa, AC/DC was seeking to keep it LOUD as always. Angus explained to *Guitar Player* that, in spite of the fast-rising tide of hair metal, 'we never thought of ourselves as a "heavy metal band". We've always regarded ourselves as a rock band. The big difference is we've always thought we had a lot more feel for rock – we always went out for songs, not riffs or heavy, heavy sounds. But every now and again it does come on like a sledgehammer.'

FOR THOSE ABOUT TO ROCK (WE SALUTE YOU) (1981)

This time that sledgehammer would come in the form of the album's cannons, which came, as Angus explained in an interview with journalist Paul Cashmere, when 'we were looking for something at the time the royal wedding with Charles and Di was going on. We were in Paris putting down demo tracks for that album. When we were doing that song we just stopped and we could hear the cannons going off. One of the guys had the TV on of the royal wedding. I said it sounded great so let's try that.'

Though the band had quickly decided on Paris as the place to track their eighth studio album (and second with Brian Johnson), the process of getting started wasn't as simple as just booking a studio and hitting the record button. Not with a band of the sonic dynamics of AC/DC, nor with a producer as methodical as Mutt Lange. For, as simple as their music was perceived coming out of the speakers or offstage by critics and fans, the science of recording those sounds in a studio was far more complicated, as Brian Johnson described in an interview with rock journalist Paul Stenning. 'We came to Paris and went into EMI Pathé Marconi Studios, which must be a good studio because a lot of bands use it, but it just wasn't right for us ... We went in thinking it was OK, but, when we tried to get that live sound we wanted on the album, it just didn't happen.'

Alternatives were in very short supply: engineer Mark

Dearnley said that, even ahead of the band trying out that studio, he and Lange had 'pretty much tried out every studio in town trying to find the right place for them. All of the studios we'd tried were just too dead to match the picture Mutt had in his head for a live, ambient type of sound, and studios at that time were pretty much designed to kill ambience. In the end, we wound up in the stone rehearsal room of H.I.S., and Mutt brought up Mobile One recording studio from London.'

According to Gearslutz.com, the concept for The Rolling Stones Mobile Studio came about in 1968 when the band decided they needed a new environment in which to record. 'Tired of the 9-to-5 limitations of a regular studio, the Stones decided to use Mick Jagger's new country house [Stargroves, in rural Berkshire] to record new music. All the necessary equipment had to be brought to the house, so the idea of putting a control room into a van was brought up by their road manager Ian Stewart.'

'Under Stewart's guidance, a variety of top engineers and producers, including Glyn Johns, were consulted in the project's creation, which was then taken to Dick Swettenham's company Helios Electronics. Known for making mixing consoles for some of the most exclusive studios of the time, the company then produced the first working version of The Rolling Stones Mobile Studio. Originally only intended for use by The Stones, the unit soon gained popularity among the likes of other classic bands, such as The Who, The Faces and Led Zeppelin.'

'From the beginning the Mobile Studio was quite experimental. It was the first fully fitted mobile multi-track studio, and could be adapted to whatever specifications the job required. When recording orchestral music for the Frank Zappa film *200 Motels*, problems arose when the silver aluminium body kept showing up in the background of the film. The entire unit was then painted with a camouflage colour scheme to hide it in the trees. It sported this look for many years to come. Originally the unit supported a maximum of 20 microphones and had an eight-channel recording format. As the Mobile began to be used for live recording, the eight-channel format quickly proved insufficient and an upgrade to 16-track took place.'

Essentially, the mobile mirrored the equipment that the Rolling Stones had used while recording *Sticky Fingers* in the South of France. Producer-engineer Andy Johns recalled that, before the Rolling Stones Mobile, 'there were things like the Pie unit, which I recorded Led Zeppelin and Ginger Baker on, which was just a bunch of equipment in the back of a van, that you'd take in, set up in a dressing room and run cables with an eight-track. Now I don't know whose idea this was, but it was a very clever idea: they put the recording unit inside of a Bedford truck, so we could go anywhere and record anywhere.'

'On the *Sticky Fingers* record, Mick had bought this house

called Stargroves – funny he would buy a place … which had no furniture, because they had no money. No one had any money back then – no furniture, a bed, a chair. Huge room, nothing except a few futons. Because they were broke – they were always broke then – but the truck worked!'

Back in Paris, AC/DC were going for the same live vibe while keeping what *Guitar Player* described as their 'power-in-simplicity formula' intact. 'We had lots of equipment there for *For Those About to Rock*,' Angus told the same publication. 'We brought in a mobile, and recorded in a big rehearsal room to see what we could get away with.'

Delving into how the album's thunderous sounds were captured, engineer Dearnley explained, 'For the drums on that album, we had a PA set up, so we had it feeding back into the drum kit on that one. We had kick and snare mics fed through the PA, feeding extra ring back into the drum kit, so it was like an extra resonance. Of course, it was almost set to the verge of feedback, so, if a snare drum dropped a little bit, we suddenly got some feedback flying around. Miking those drums, I remember we used a KM-84 on the snare drum, and the reason I remember that is because we kept blowing up heads on it, so new capsules had to be sent down from England on a regular basis. That was Mutt's favourite mic, and turned out to be the sound, so the poor Neumann took a beating on that particular album. Because there was so much ambience flowing around, we didn't need any room mics –

there was really enough room going on in the overheads of the drums on that.'

The album's basic tracks were recorded live off the floor as usual. 'That's the only way you can get that feeling happening,' Angus told *Guitar Player*. 'We always do all the back tracks together – the two guitars, the bass and drums.'

The same group approach followed with songwriting, as Angus explained to *Guitar Player*. 'The three of us – me, Brian and Malcolm – get together and just thrash out whatever we've got. If I've any ideas in the tape or something, I'll play them; Malcolm the same. We'll combine them all. Every now and again he might have something really good and I'll say, "What if you try this?" Or he'll say to me, "I want you to sing something here if you can," and I'll try to think of something. The song can start from anywhere –it can be a riff or a title. Brian could say, "I've got a good line here," and suddenly it might inspire something.'

From there, Dearnley recalled, 'The lyrics were finalised in the studio, but Malcolm and Angus had come in with all of the songs musically finished.'

Angus told journalist Stenning that the inspiration for the album's title track stemmed from the sheer power of the music. 'We had this chorus riff and we thought, "Well, this sounds rather deadly." We were trying to find a good title and there's this book from years ago about Roman gladiators called *For Those About to Die We Salute You*. So we thought *For*

Those About to Rock... I mean, it sounds better than *"For those about to die"*. Actually, that song's got a lot of meaning to it. It's a very inspiring song. It makes you feel a bit powerful and I think that's what rock 'n' roll is all about.'

Discussing some of the album's other titles with the same journalist, Brian Johnson summed up 'Inject the Venom' by singling out the line 'that says, "If you inject the venom it will be your last attack," which is like a snake. Once it bites you, it's got nothing left.'

'It's rather like the title track,' Angus added. 'It means: "Have it hot." Do it once, do it hard and good or you're finished. It's a real rock 'n' roll line.'

Of 'Let's Get it Up', which pays their usual homage to their female fans, Brian quipped that the song could be summed up as filth. 'Pure filth. We're a filthy band!'

Turning to the track 'Spellbound', Brian Johnson said that the song was 'about when you get one of those days when it's like a trance. It's hard to describe really but that's "Spellbound". We set it to a man driving a car, blinded by a bright beam. But it could be any situation. I'm sure there's some deep Americans who can tell you what we're talking about.'

Angus added that the song's groove was 'a slower one for us but we liked it anyhow. It's one of those moody ones. It's so simple; it's like being naughty. Like peeking through the keyhole at somebody changing their knickers or something. Nothing bad. We're just pranksters more than anything. You're having fun and that's all there is.'

Reflecting on the band's rebellious attitude towards any convention except their own, Angus laid out the thinking behind 'Breaking the Rules' as a response to any time 'when someone says, "You can't do that."They were always saying that to me at school. You do it anyhow.'

As usual, the band's brighter rock anthems were balanced out by the darker lyrical territory of tracks like 'Evil Walks' and 'C.O.D.'. With the former, Angus explained to Stenning, 'As the name says, evil walks – it's everywhere! When we were playing it at the beginning I said, "Those chords sounds dead evil." And that's how we do it, just sitting around and nattering and jamming away. And someone says something like "evil walks" and that's it.'

'C.O.D.', Angus revealed, had a different meaning to what people might expect. 'Most people think of C.O.D. as a "cash on delivery" or "cash on demand". I was sitting around trying to come up with a better one, and I came up with "Care of the Devil". But we're not black magic Satanists or whatever you call it. I don't drink blood. I may wear black underwear now and then but that's about it.'

When attention turned to laying the album's blistering guitar tracks, engineer Dearnley recalled that, in line with the band's formula for playing rock 'n' roll, 'the recording technique didn't change a great deal with them – it was pretty much the 57s on the guitars, and an AKG 120 a little farther back'.

Angus shed some light on the band's guitar-playing techniques when he talked about his brother Malcolm's rhythmic role in the band. 'He makes it look so simple,' the lead guitarist told *Guitar Player*. 'There are people out there who do that, and you look at them and what they make, that is their art. They make the hard look simple.'

He was more humble when discussing his own playing style, dismissing the dizzying lead magic he laid over the top of Malcolm's rhythms as 'the easiest part, the solos. There is no great thing in being a solo artist. The hardest thing is to play with a lot of people together, and to do it right. I mean, when all four guys hit the one note at once, very few people can do that.'

Elaborating a bit more on the science of soloing, he explained to *Guitar Player* that, when laying down any solo in the studio, 'I just want to add to the song. I don't want to take away from it. You don't want to suddenly give a raging solo in a song where really it should be sitting in there. Sometimes it can go over the top. Guys will try to get in every lick they can get, cover every bit of space. We just like to go with what the track requires.'

From the vantage point of the engineer, Mark Dearnley celebrated Angus's talent for spontaneity, calling it 'a wonderful thing, no matter how long it takes. Angus has the ability to be spontaneous and very musical at the same time – not everyone has that talent. With some of the other guitarists I've recorded, it's better to have a formed part, but Angus just blows a few takes off, and perhaps he might combine a part of one with part of another. That said, while he probably had a picture in his head, I wouldn't expect to hear the same part over and over. He would get the basic plots, then knock it off, sitting on the sofa, radio mic, feet up, cig in his mouth – most unlike what you see on stage.'

Once the band had completed laying the album's backing tracks, they moved to Family Sound Studios to track Brian's vocals and Angus's guitar overdubs. Dearnley underscored their tightness as a musical entity by pointing out that – unlike most groups – throughout the entirety of the album's recording, 'the band was an absolutely locked-together unit, and everybody was in the studio for everything. It was a case of spending three months having a vacation and having to make a record at the same time – it was that sort of atmosphere. It wasn't a very lengthy process really. Although we ended up spending more time making records, it wasn't because we spent more time in the studio recording – we spent a lot of time chatting.'

When Brian did step up to the microphone to record, Dearnley felt fortunate to have the advantage of familiarity with his singing style. 'Before Brian even joined the band, I had worked on an album with him in his first band, Geordie, which was recorded at Lansdowne with John McSwift as engineer, and me as assistant. So, when Brian came into the studio, we had some history, and I was already familiar with Brian's style.

'We used a 67 for Brian. The great thing about that mic is they have a clarity, and a little bit more in the bottom end. When you have a vocalist like Brian who sings at the very top of his range all the time, you need as much of the warmth as you can get out of the mic. So it tends to be a pretty good workhorse mic for singers like Bon and Brian.' The only problem in the vocal recording process came, he recalled, when 'occasionally he'd have trouble because it was such a top-range thing that it would be fairly tiring to sing at that level for any length of time'.

At the end of September 1981, after the main tracking on the album had been completed, the album's crowning, signature touch was added with the firing of the infamous cannon that adorns the LP's cover. In an interview with rock journalist Ethan Schlesinger, Malcolm quipped, 'If it was a real cannon out there and we could blow everyone's brains out, then that would be GREAT!'

Dearnley, however, admitted it was a sound effect he did later. 'While I'd love to have said we got a cannon and recorded it, it was an overdub.'

Once recording had wrapped, drummer Phil Rudd celebrated by buying a BMW M1. 'He decided to show me how fast it would go around the periphery of Paris,' Dearnley remembered, 'which was very much a brown trouser experience! With AC/DC, I was just happy to be part of it all.'

Released on 23 November 1981, *For Those About to Rock (We Salute You)* was the band's first album to reach No. 1 in the United States, spawning hit singles with 'For Those About to Rock' and 'Let's Get It Up,' and solidifying the band's position. Seeming quite comfortable in the knowledge that 'we're never going to win any Grammy awards', Brian Johnson told journalist Stenning that his ultimate goal with any AC/DC album was to 'keep on doing ... whatever I did on *Back in Black* ... It sold 12 million albums and I'm chuffed to bits! But with the new one, you can never be complacent. You can't sit back and say, "Hey, the last one worked." It's still up to the kids whether they buy it or tell you to piss off and try again – "Don't try to bullshit us."'

With *For Those About to Rock...* the band delivered to its fans a solid AC/DC album of which the *Village Voice* wisely observed, 'I recommend you go get it.'

CHAPTER EIGHT

FLICK OF THE SWITCH
(1983)

'It's a really difficult thing to do with a band that's as
basic as AC/DC – to try and make them sound
different – because they don't. The only reference point
we had was that BB King "Mannish Boy" recording
that Johnny Winter made where you can hear
everything in the room'
TONY PLATT, ENGINEER

Following the solid performance of *For Those About to
Rock*... AC/DC were eager to continue the momentum
they'd been building but found it frustrating that they had to
wait for producer Mutt Lange to get all the sounds worked out
to perfection. 'It was taking too long,' Malcolm Young told
Mojo. 'He was trying to outdo *Back in Black* for sound, and it was
the sound he was looking for, whereas we were thinking of the
music – and the performances were starting to suffer... We
found ourselves getting trapped by producers who wanted
something different from us, so this time we thought, "Bollocks
to them – we'll do it."

'We did that one so quickly and I guess it was a reaction to

For Those About to Rock,' he added to rock journalist Susan Masino. 'We just thought, "Bugger it! We've had enough of this crap!" Nobody was in the mood to spend another year making a record, so we decided to produce it ourselves and make sure it was as raw as AC/DC could be.'

Angus echoed his brother's sentiments, explaining afterwards to *Guitar Player* that they wanted it raw. 'We always were raw sounding; we just wanted it more free of the reverbs and the effects. You like a natural drum sound – you don't want this gigantic echo going on. A lot of people go, "What is that?" because sometimes it sounds like oil drums or something. We tend to go for keeping the raw idea of it all, because that's really what rock music is meant to sound like.'

In undertaking such a monumental responsibility – especially given the long shadow cast by Mutt Lange – the band invited engineer Tony Platt back to record the album for them. 'When we got to *Flick of the Switch*, I think they wanted to have somebody in the room they could trust,' he recalled. 'I was supposed to engineer *For Those About to Rock*, but there was a mix-up in scheduling and I'd already started doing another album. The guy who was managing AC/DC hadn't made the dates clear to everybody. So, for the next album, they invited me back to engineer and the band produced themselves.'

Feeling that they'd worked hard for their freedom in the studio, Angus revealed in an interview with *The Aquarian* (a

New Jersey alternative newspaper) that 'we had to do a lot of battling for what we wanted. Malcolm took care of a lot of the songs on that album, because Mutt didn't really understand them.'

Talking to rock journalist Paul Stenning, Angus offered fans some insight into the brothers' writing process. 'Usually I start a few weeks after we've gotten off the road. I'll tell everyone not to bother me because I don't want to know anything about rock 'n' roll for a while. But after about two weeks, I find myself drawn to the same old battered SG that I've been playing for years, and I start to play certain chords. Before I know it, a great deal of a song is written. That's when Malcolm or Brian will come in and help me finish off. It's really a very simple process. I guess you could say I write most of the songs out of boredom.'

Of brother Malcolm's contributions, Angus added, 'I can churn out hundreds of riffs. But [he] will come up with one and once you hear it, you'll go, "Shit!" He has that classic guitar feel, like in a song like "Back in Black" or "Fly on the Wall". A lot of people don't appreciate what rhythm is.'

For his own part, Malcolm told Paul Stenning that, as far as the band was concerned, consistency was king. 'The critics might not like us – as Angus said the other day, "We put out the same record every year with a different cover!" – but the kids still like it, and that's all we're worried about.'

In recording the album, engineer Platt's chief concern

centred on who was going to call the shots. 'If there was any difficulty that came with the band self-producing, it was I didn't have the authority in the room. There was nobody like Mutt with the authority in the room to say, "That's good, that's bad, we should change that," or "We should stop there now." That said, even as engineer, I was doing much the same things Mutt had been doing on previous albums: making sure the lyrics were working and the songs were working in terms of arrangement, and so on and so forth. In some respects, it was a very difficult job to do, because again I was having to take on some of the production roles without the authority – and to be careful at the same time of not rubbing people the wrong way.'

As far as the band was concerned, the music they were making while recording *Flick of the Switch* was working because AC/DC's music first and foremost embraced the philosophy of keeping things simple. 'We've got the basic things kids want,' Angus explained to Stenning. 'They want to rock, and that's it.'

Malcolm told the same writer, 'People can go out and hear R.E.M. if they want deep lyrics, but at the end of the night they want to go home and get fucked! That's where AC/DC comes into it.'

AC/DC's writing process for *Flick of the Switch* began, as far as Malcolm was concerned, with the band relying 'on the beat'. Angus added to journalist Masino that the Young brothers have always liked music 'because it's simple and direct – you don't have to think about it. It makes you dance and tap your feet. I've never been impressed with someone who can zoom up and down [the guitar neck]. I can do that myself, but I call it practising.'

Elaborating on the specific guitar sound he was pursuing for his signature scorching solos, Angus explained to Stenning, 'It's just how you hear it in your mind. You try to stick to it because a lot of people get condemned for not doing it. If you can do it, it's always good to throw something in, but still keep that feeling in there. You don't want the kids to come in and say, "Aw, that guy is trying to play Beethoven on top of that sound."'

On the same topic, Angus told *Guitar Player* that he prefers to track his solos 'usually when [the] mind is clear. If your mind is totally blank on what you're doing, then you just go and do it.' Again he paid tribute to Malcolm's judgement, adding that he had been known to ask for another take on those occasions where 'he thinks they're not happening – if he thinks they're not rock enough or don't suit the song. It's mainly the songs that we worry about. I won't sit there and spend 12 hours on a guitar solo. I couldn't. That's pointless. I like to go in and just go, bang away at it.'

From the technical side, however, engineer Tony Platt still harboured mixed feelings about the lack of a producer. 'I don't think it was a mistake for the band to self-produce the album, just a set of circumstances that didn't come together in the right way. I'm always reluctant to try and analyse that album – it was a difficult time for the band for a lot of reasons. In a lot of respects, the album was just a victim of circumstance.

'First off, we went back to Compass Point Studios in Nassau, and we set everything up the same way we had for *Back in Black*. From a production standpoint, I thought it was exactly the right thing to do, because I thought *For Those About to Rock* had lost something that *Back in Black* had. So, in one respect, the attempt to actually just find out what that component was, and go the same route we had on *Back in Black* was not a bad thing. And in fact what we got was something sonically that was pretty close to *Back in Black*.'

Self-production, however, can be 'a double-edged sword', as Platt could see with hindsight. 'Because when you're tracking AC/DC, it's just straightforward really – you just have to record them in the most honest way possible. If you record them honestly, and everything isn't quite right, then you record the bad as well as the good bits.'

When attention turned to mixing, Platt felt he was making a safe bet with Electric Ladyland Studios, where he had mixed both *Back in Black* and *For Those About to Rock* at the same desk. Still, after listening to the first mixes for *Flick of the Switch*, the engineer remembered feeling that strategy might have been a bit off-point. 'The first set of mixes – after checking them out on Cliff Williams's portable stereo system at the hotel – having done the first two or three mixes, Cliff turned around and said, "Wow, this sounds like an extension of *Back in Black*." So then the notion started to get put around that, "Well, maybe we should try and make this sound different," so we carried on the mixing but I started trying to use a different approach, to have it sound different from both *Back in Black* and *For Those About to Rock*. That was the mistake I think – I don't think that was a good thing to do at all.'

Still, the band was pleased with the results, as Brian Johnson told Stenning. 'The album is a really good rock album, that's all it is. We weren't trying to do anything else – we just wanted another album that would burn! It's a little different this time, because we didn't have a producer, but that turned out to be an advantage. It was like, we had our own thoughts and there was no outside influence to stop us. It was a struggle at times to produce ourselves but that was half the fun of it.'

Ultimately, the band walked away from the experience happy with what they had created, and the critics agreed. *Blender* magazine's overview was that the experiment had been a success: 'AC/DC responded to the early-'80s hair-metal trend by ditching producer "Mutt" Lange and returning to the raw blues of their early days.' *Brave Words/Bloody Knuckles* magazine rated it as 'their most underrated album' and hailed it as a 'back-to-basics Young brothers-produced [album] … that sears with flailing axes and raw intrigue. A real beauty.' *Kerrang!* would declare that 'no album after 1983's *Flick of the Switch* has quite matched the energy and excitement of the band's blistering live shows' – something that reflected the band's own feeling.

'There's a whole new excitement about this band these days,' Angus told journalist Masino, 'and there's a whole new generation of kids to be won over.'

Sadly, following the release of *Flick of the Switch*, drummer Phil Rudd made the decision to leave the band. The reason behind his departure, he said in an interview with *Rock Hard France*, was that 'the whole recording process ... literally drained me'.

But the true root of his emptiness, in Angus's opinion, really lay somewhere in his still unresolved feelings about the group following the death of Bon Scott. 'The biggest change I saw in him was when Bon died,' he told Stenning. 'He couldn't take it so well because, as a band, things had been that tight between us, it was pretty thick. We had done a lot together; lived in a house together, set up all the gear together, slept with the same women – at the same time! When Bon died, it hit him harder than anyone. He really thought that I in particular wouldn't be doing it any more. So, when we carried on, he thought that the early thing – the tightness – had gone, which wasn't the case.'

In an interview with the Californian radio station KNAC,

Malcolm added his opinion that, by that point, Phil was 'burned out'.

Looking back years later, Rudd – in an interview with a British newspaper – would conclude, 'We had been together for too long. After a while, you kind of lose the plot. It wasn't the music.'

CHAPTER NINE

FLY ON THE WALL
(1985)

AC/DC's tenth studio album in as many years was a change of pace for the band on several fronts. Perhaps the most significant of these was the decision to replace Phil Rudd with Dio beat-keeper Simon Wright, who had responded to an anonymous advertisement in *Sounds* music weekly for a 'hard hitting rock 'n' roll drummer ... Any other crap need not apply.'

Simon had had no idea he was walking into a try-out for hard rock's biggest band, as he recalled to journalist Murray Engleheart. 'The audition was with the drum tech, Dickie Jones. The drum kit was set up, and you had to play three songs. I think it was Led Zeppelin, ZZ Top and AC/DC. And luckily for me, I'd been playing all of these songs. I sort of figured it might be a good gig because of where it was being held, because it's quite a fancy rehearsal studio. There wasn't much reaction really – I just finished and Dickie said, "That's great – we'll definitely be in touch with you." And I think a day later they got in touch and said, "You wanna come back and play?" I still didn't know what band it was for.'

'So I go back and I'm walking down the corridor and there's flight cases with AC/DC all over... and I'm like "Oh my GOD! You gotta be kidding! It can't be them!" And I get shown in and say hello to Angus, Mal and Cliff. Brian wasn't there. I was shitting myself, you know? But they were really nice – they were great, made me feel comfortable. And we just played and that was it really. I got the call a couple days later.'

Explaining why Wright was the right choice for AC/DC, Malcolm Young told *Metal CD* that 'he knew what he was doing and we just had to guide him in the right direction and leave him to get on with the job. It's a very simple thing, playing drums for AC/DC, but sometimes it can be hard to keep it simple.' In another vote of confidence he added in an interview with *Record Review*, 'If we'd heard him back when we were first forming, he would have been a contender to be our drummer then.'

Recording began in October 1984 at Mountain Studios in Montreux, Switzerland, against the backdrop of the Alps. Sharing his impressions of the studio where he'd lay his first drum tracks with the band, Simon described the studio as amazing. 'It was this huge casino on Lake Geneva. And there was smoke on the water. That's the same one [as the song by Deep Purple]. It was a huge round room and it was all sectioned off with little huts and stuff where they'd put the amps and isolate. To get up to the control room there was this section of stairs like a fire escape kinda thing.'

'The guys actually went down a ladder into this big circular room from the studio control room to record,' confirmed engineer Mark Dearnley, describing the casino ballroom where the band tracked live off its floor. 'It was a very large, live room, which sounded great through the Neve console they had, which was a very nice desk.'

Detailing its history – the facility was originally owned by Queen's Freddie Mercury – the studio says, 'Since 1975, the famous Mountain Recording Studios [has been] located in Montreux, Switzerland within the walls of the modern casino building. This … sound facility, designed by Westlake Audio Inc. of Los Angeles, was without question the most modern, sophisticated and best equipped sound facility in Europe. Mountain Studios recorded some of the greatest, most legendary musicians of our time.'

House engineer David Richards added in a 1987 interview that 'Mountain … has a nice old Neve console with Studer 48-track tape machines.'

As for the musical approach for the new project, Angus explained to *Metal CD* that he felt he and Malcolm could best capture on tape the sounds they were hearing in their heads.

'We wanted to pick it up a bit more for this album, so we tried our hands at producing it ourselves again, but putting some more time and thought into what we were doing instead of just taping ourselves.'

Remembering an easy-going environment during recording, engineer Dearnley felt that 'Angus and Malcolm producing was absolutely fine, because everybody in the band knew their roles, so there weren't any heads butting. I felt part of that team in exactly the same manner as the band – I knew what they did, they knew what I did – and so there was never that conflict. Everybody respected each other's jobs.'

In an interview with *Guitar Player*, Angus cited the brothers' creative intuition as probably their greatest strength working in the studio. 'I just think as brothers you can sort of shout each other down. You can go, "Hey, cut that out!" So you've just got a good rapport. Malcolm does inspire me. He has very high standards in his way of playing and everything. He's very musical-minded, but he can go to the extremes. Like if we are in a studio and I have to do these things like solos, he'll say, "I want this to rock like thunder," and you've got to make it rock. He just says something like that and you know exactly what he means.'

That innate understanding of the band's musical foundations also extended to knowing what their fans wanted to hear on an AC/DC album. Angus knew they should not stray too far from their musical homestead, and reasoned in an interview with *Guitar Player* that 'most other people can sort of just go bang, bang, bang – there's a song and that's the end of it. They forget having that sort of style they can stick to. Most bands in the world can chop and change their style into anything. They can do reggae, they can do slow – we can't. We have that style of playing, that's what we do best. You can write songs, but it mightn't be AC/DC, so you have to think of that all the time.'

Brian Johnson elaborated further in an interview with journalist Paul Stenning. 'When I'm singing it and the lads are playing it, you know that is just rock 'n' roll, a way to put it across. You've got to go right over the fucking top. Like everything – big gear, big lights, big fucking sound, and that's how it is … I'm an out and out basic man and AC/DC are one of the best rock 'n' roll bands in the world, doing things just to the basics.'

With tracking under way in the casino ballroom annexe at Mountain Studios, Dearnley described the continuity between the 'ambient feel we were going for and the very ambient room' in which the band was tracking. 'The miking set-up was pretty much the same as past albums I'd done with the band. The whole AC/DC thing with the drums are kick and snare, and there's not really room for the drummer to be clever, or rarely – he's just part of the steam engine cranking forward. I remember, after the second day of tracking, Simon got shouted at for putting in a drum fill, but that was about it.'

After laying the album's solo overdubs with his trusty Gibson SG, Angus talked about his soloing technique to *Guitar Player*. 'I never had an ear for sitting and picking out notes,' he said. 'I just play it. If you said to me, "Play someone else's song," and I did it, you'd go "What's he playing?" I can't sit down and pick a note off a record. Mal's got a good ear for hearing things, but me, I never did. I always think it's more the feeling. If you ever got an album where they included a couple of different takes, like an old blues album, you'll hear it. The one they settle for in the end usually has a different feeling and sounds totally different. I never work them out before, unless there's an important part, like if it's part of the song. It just has to flow. Solos have got to have continuity.'

Upon wrapping production, the band seemed happy with an album but for the first time in the band's career critics and fans would feel a bit less impassioned about it. The *Village Voice* concluded that *Fly on the Wall* was 'an unremarkable but hardly terrible AC/DC album', while *Billboard* magazine – in a barely complimentary tone – noted that 'as with nearly every AC/DC album, there are a few good songs, notably "Shake Your Foundations" and "Sink the Pink"'. By contrast, the *Miami New Times* celebrated these two singles as 'among the most killer songs the band has ever recorded' and hailed the album as 'Goddamn awesome'.

The band seemed to take a philosophical stance on this mixed reception, with Angus reasoning in an interview with *Guitar Player* that 'everybody goes up and down. We just try to play our music and not worry about anything else. *Back in Black* is our most successful album in the States so many of our fans base their expectations on that. But we were around long before *Back in Black*. In America people tend to associate wealth with success, whereas in other parts of the world success has more to do with making something that satisfies you.'

Mark Dearnley offered the further observation that 'it's the classic thing where the band had had two mega-multi-platinum sellers back to back with *Highway to Hell* and *Back in Black*, which itself had sold almost 20 million copies by that point I think. Against that backdrop, a single- or double-platinum seller after that is regarded as a bit of a failure.'

Brian Johnson also gave his perspective on criticism to *Kerrang!*. 'The first thing Angus and Malcolm said to me when I joined this band – they said, "Do you mind if your feelings ever get hurt?" And I said, "Why?" And they said, "Because if you're going to join this band, you're going to be expected to take fucking stick. Because we've been slagged off by every fucking reporter since we left Australia." And I said, "Well, I'm going to have to take stick anyway, taking this lad's place." But luckily these guys are so much like a fucking family that you never get the chance to feel alone;

like you could just sit by yourself in your hotel room and feel like shit. The lads say to me, "Just fucking ignore them." We're good in our field. We just out and out don't give a fuck. We play what we play and that's it. And the good thing is, no one else can do it as good as this band. The band is the fucking best!'

Indeed, regardless of lacklustre sales in the context of *Back in Black or Highway to Hell*, Angus Young was ever appreciative of the fans. 'There has always been someone we've been packaged with, but AC/DC, we have always looked at ourselves as a rock 'n' roll band. From the moment we started, it was always a compliment that you could motivate somebody to part with his hard-earned money and walk into a record shop and buy your record ... Our music makes me jump up and down ... I hope people use the music as fun, to have a party and get out their AC/DC records!'

CHAPTER TEN

WHO MADE WHO (1986)/
BLOW UP YOUR VIDEO
(1988)

**'I've always liked Chuck Berry's music because
it's simple and direct. You don't have to think about it.
It makes you dance and tap your feet'**
ANGUS YOUNG

The death of Bon Scott aside, if ever AC/DC had a need of a comeback, it came in the nick of time with 'Who Made Who', the band's first smash single since 'For Those About to Rock…'. As Brian Johnson recalled to rock journalist Paul Stenning, 'In the middle '80s, we had a bit of a bad time when all the music changed, long hairs… you know, Whitesnake and REO Speedwagon. The record company came to us to tell us to change the clothes – they said, "It would be best if you would change your image." We were like, "Fuck you!" And all the bands that did change aren't here any more. Because they let themselves be manipulated by the record companies, who quite frankly don't have a clue about music. They have only one thing: they know how to make money out of music. But that's it, that's where it all ends. It's a funny world.'

Sticking to the four-on-the-floor style that had kept them atop the hard-rock mountain for more than a decade, AC/DC mounted their second commercial comeback in a decade when legendary horror author Stephen King approached the band about using highlights from their catalogue as the soundtrack to *Maximum Overdrive*, a new film he was writing and directing. The songs involved were 'You Shook Me All Night Long', 'Sink the Pink', 'Ride On', 'Hells Bells', 'Shake Your Foundations' and 'For Those About to Rock (We Salute You)', along with two newly tracked instrumentals, 'D.T.' and 'Chase the Ace'.

The band added the wrinkle that they produce an original single to accompany the soundtrack's release, which turned out to be 'Who Made Who'. King, who plays in a rock band of his own, seemed thrilled that the band had accepted his invitation, stating proudly at the time, 'I like rhythm 'n' blues, I like rock 'n' roll. AC/DC I like a *lot* – very loud!'

All the chosen songs were simple, straightforward and highly accessible. Elaborating on the sound science behind *Who Made Who*'s rhythm-friendly feel, Angus told the *International Herald Tribune* that 'it probably goes back to our roots. At the time, music was very soft and we wanted something that was more popular. When you're in the bar, the music people liked most — and would get up and dance and have a good time to — was loud rock music. I always thought there's something going on here, because, when they put on a love song, people sat it out. But when you put on a rock track people get off their feet. I'm not a psychologist, but I think there's something of a primal beat that sits inside us all, and the public seems to like music when it has more energy.'

The band made a further acknowledgement of their roots by going back to their old writing and production team of Harry Vanda and George Young for the new title track, 'Who Made Who'. Ever-down-to-earth, Malcolm observed, 'I think [it] was what we needed. "Who Made Who" was a return to form for the band.'

Recording the instrumentals for the movie, however, proved something of a strange experience, as drummer Simon Wright recalled. 'We had these TV screens which showed us the relevant parts of the movie, and we had to fit the music to the action.'

In addition to the soundtrack's rock numbers, Angus told *Metal Creem*, 'We ended up doing everything, all the horror noises and everything. All the Hollywood stuff!'

On the soundtrack's release on 24 May 1986, Angus seemed particularly proud of what the band had accomplished in the studio. 'I think we've done a good job and we achieved what we wanted,' he told *Guitar Player*. 'We just wanted to make a tough and exciting rock 'n' roll record. And that's what we made.'

Riding high on the success of 'Who Made Who', which *Billboard* confirmed 'put the band right back on track commercially', the band's first film soundtrack went on to sell over five million copies, the biggest numbers the band had moved in years. Shortly afterwards, they began plotting their next album – a return to the sonic basics that had first made them pilots of the hard-rock genre. They were going to enter the studio with big brother George Young, who was riding high with the band off the success of 'Who Made Who'.

Elaborating on the decision, Angus told Stenning, 'I always think that we did the great rock tunes when we worked with my brother. I like what we did with him better than the stuff we did with Mutt Lange. Mutt was very conscious of what was popular in America but with my brother … if it was a rock 'n' roll song, he made sure it rocked.'

Once again AC/DC returned to Compass Point Studios. As Brian explained, the studio where the band record always plays a big part. 'We need a place that's got a *great* live sound. We're not looking for technology, like effects and stuff. We rely mainly on getting the best sound out of whatever room we're in.'

Angus added that the band felt Nassau was an ideal place for them to lock themselves away to work, explaining to writer Stenning that 'it's actually very slow at Compass Point. I mean, the studio itself is very good but the lifestyle is such that you tend to spend half the day lying around on the beach and having to work at night. But we didn't do that. Once we started working we wanted to get on.'

As for how the Bahamas affected crafting the album's songs, Angus told Stenning, 'I don't think there is an ideal environment for writing songs. We've written songs under a hell of a lot of pressure, but then some songs just come suddenly and spontaneously, like when you're not thinking and you're in the middle of a cab ride. We've even written songs on stage. The key, I suppose, never knowing when to expect it.'

Angus also identified this element of serendipity as a fundamental feature of anything the band laid in the studio. 'When we write songs the first thing is to feel … We're still as tough as ever and there's definitely no ballads. I have a great aversion to slow songs. Apart from anything else the world is saturated with the damn things. I don't mind hearing a ballad every now and then, like once a year maybe, but even then I get pissed off after about two minutes. So, whatever we try in the studio, it won't be a ballad! … It's got to have that bottom edge to it and you take it from there. It's dumb to make a song fast just for the sake of it.'

As always, Angus's biggest sounding board for his guitar solos was Malcolm, who Angus credited as a big inspiration.

'He can always tell me if I'm playing good or bad,' he told Stenning. 'He's a very tough critic. I know if I can please Malcolm I can please the world. A lot of people say, "AC/DC – that's the band with the little guy who runs around in shorts." But I wouldn't be able to do it without Malcolm and the other guys pumping out the rhythm. That makes me good.'

Another aid came in the form of Angus's trusty Marshall stack, which he preferred set very clean. 'A lot of people who have picked up my guitar and tried it through my amp have been shocked at how clean it is. They think it's a very small sound when they play it and wonder how it sounds so much bigger when I'm playing. I just like enough gain so that it will still cut when you hit a lead lick without getting that sort of false Tonebender-type sound. I like to get natural sustain from a guitar and amp.'

Discussing the amount of volume distortion he liked from the amp, he added, 'it just depends on the nature of the room. If you've got a great-sounding live room and everyone's in the same room, especially the drums and the guitars, then I think you'll really cook because there's more of a feeling of camaraderie. It makes for much more of a live feel. If you're in the control room or separated, sometimes you can be a little bit cut off. We've done it different ways, but a lot of it is still down to the room itself. If you've got a great-sounding live room, you can get lucky.'

Brian Johnson painted the recording as something akin to a family backyard barbeque instead of making an album. 'We just went through the whole album with smiles on our faces,' he told a British journalist. 'The album is smashing, and we just knew it was going to be good. George has this father-figure approach and he knows more about rock 'n' roll than any fucker! Then you've got Malcolm and Angus there, so happy to work with their own brother, and Harry [Vanda] too!'

The singer added of the sessions' success that 'with the three brothers working together, I think it's just the climax of many years of doing the right thing with music. What I love to watch sometimes is Mal or Ang will look at George and just go "ummm". And George will go "hmmm". They've just had a conversation! But it was through the mind, without words getting in the way. I think the boys believe in George more than anybody in the world. They trust him. I do too.'

In a conversation with *Brave Words / Bloody Knuckles*, Malcolm said, 'We just try hard to please ourselves really. You gotta do what you do best. You get lots of people saying, "Oh, when are they gonna change?" and plenty say, "Don't change." We couldn't change 'cause we only know the stuff we like — straight ahead rock 'n' roll, no frills and good performances. The music really is the important thing — that's the bottom line. Personally, that's all I'm interested in. I'm not even much up for the rest of the thrills of it.'

Happily, the sound that most pleased the band had the same effect on their fans, who soon put *Blow Up Your Video* in the Billboard Top 200 Album Chart on its release on 18 January 1988. Quickly certified double-platinum, the album produced the hit 'Heatseeker', which *Blender* hailed as 'their best song in years', while *Rolling Stone* reported that *Blow Up Your Video* became their biggest-selling album since *For Those About to Rock* and set the stage for the band's 1990s renaissance.

CHAPTER ELEVEN
THE RAZORS EDGE
(1990)

'From our background, we were always a band
that tried to make a good album. We concentrated on
that. Where other bands made pop music or changed
their direction, we always stuck to what we do
best, which is rock music'
ANGUS YOUNG

Following a decade of the ups and downs that follow the
kind of zenith the band had reached with *Back in Black*,
by 1990 AC/DC had built back up to fulfilling their creative
potential with the release of *The Razors Edge*. Right from the
album's opening notes, it showed riffs as sharp as the band's
last commercial peak in 1980. *Entertainment Weekly* would
declare that 'if you're a hard-rock addict – if raucous rock 'n'
roll intensity is what you want – this is one album that really
delivers!' *Billboard*, meanwhile, hailed it as 'arguably the
Australian headbangers' strongest album in over half a decade
… a welcome addition to AC/DC's catalogue'.

This time the band had secured as producer the Canadian
heavy hitter Bruce Fairbairn, whose past successes had

included Bon Jovi's 28-million-selling *Slippery When Wet* and Aerosmith's comeback smash *Permanent Vacation* and its Grammy-winning follow-up *Pump*. In an interview with rock journalist Martin Aston, Angus recalled that band and producer had been on the same sonic page from the first pre-production meeting. '[Usually] when I sit on that side of the world, I always think producers are going to be high-powered – you know, more business than pleasure. But Bruce was really good. I was shocked in a way because the guy said, "I want you to sound like AC/DC when you were 17."' Music to the band's ears.

Angus also told rock journalist Paul Stenning that, from day one, 'Bruce told Malcolm that he didn't want us to change AC/DC. And he didn't want us to do anything that we'd be uncomfortable with. These days it's hard to find people who are rock producers. A lot of people say they are, but, as soon as you start working with them, they'll push their ballads at you. The material was all ready to go when we got to Vancouver. Fairbairn just brought out the dynamics a bit. Bruce was a big fan of our older albums; he said he liked the excitement, rawness and lack of production on them. He wanted to capture that in-your-face sound again and did a good job doing it. There were very few overdubs.'

As excited as the band was about stepping in the studio with Fairbairn, the teaming almost didn't happen. As engineer Mike Fraser recalled, 'AC/DC had already started

Razors Edge with George Young in the UK, and there had been a family illness, so they basically had everything but vocals and lead guitar overdubs recorded. So when they got to Little Mountain, initially we thought it would be a breeze because all we had to track was Brian's leads and the other overdubs.

'Well, when Brian started singing, we quickly discovered that the keys of the songs were in the wrong key for him, so we started re-recording the guitars on them to change the key and bring it down a whole step. Well, the band liked the sound and process of that better than what they already had tracked, so we wound up doing everything again, down to even cutting two or three more drum tracks with Chris. We kept a lot of the basic bed drum tracks.'

In an early 1990s cover story, *Billboard* was offered an exclusive look inside Little Mountain Studios. 'This bustling West Coast city [Vancouver] of 1.5 million residents is on the international map largely because of one recording studio,' it reported. 'Little Mountain Studios is the storied, almost mythic facility. Bruce Fairbairn, Bob Rock and Mike Fraser are the producers, and the combination has turned Vancouver into a hard-rock mecca for Bon Jovi, Aerosmith, Motley Crue, David Lee Roth and AC/DC ... More significantly, the extraordinary track record of Little Mountain Studios ... has spurred Vancouver's growth into what is arguably Canada's foremost studio centre ... [It] continues to attract big names to the facility's two main studios that together generate $1 million in revenue annually.'

Equally important to the sonic attraction of Little Mountain Studios, as producer and manager Bob Brooks recalled, was the role of its designer, the late John Vrtacic. 'I've been asked many times following the extraordinary success track of Little Mountain Studios who I credited most if not all those hits and acclaim. It was always expected that I would name people like Bob Rock or Mike Fraser; and truly their role in the fame of the studio is known by everyone. But my answer was always swift and emphatic – John Vrtacic was the key man to that success.

'John sought perfection. He was the stickler for pre-maintenance – he actually believed in warding off Murphy's Law before it struck! – and always kept an eye toward making everything work better every time and all the time. Little Mountain was one of the first studios in the world to work with the then-new Sony 3402 tape machines and then there was all of the blood, sweat, and tears that we went through with software glitches and anything else that could go wrong. The phone and Telex bills went through the roof as John conversed with Sony about the software glitches, and he'd work crazy hours with no extra compensation to get those machines to perform as they were designed to do – working optimally in the "real" world that we lived in every day. John beat down the problems and made those machines cook!'

'One day, my receptionist called to say that there were some gentlemen in the foyer. A lot of them. And they were all Japanese. Sure enough, they were from Sony and they were in Vancouver at Little Mountain Studios not to see me, but John Vrtacic. By the way, the Japanese pronunciation of "Vrtacic" was priceless – I really wish I'd recorded it. What a meeting as they finally greeted the man that had saved Sony's technical buns. They expressed over and over their gratitude to John and to us for allowing him to actually work for Sony, and showed their gratitude by virtually giving us three $75,000 machines for next to nothing.'

'John, just the way he always was, couldn't figure out what the fuss was all about. He was just doing what he thought he was supposed to do – make everything work perfectly. John was always so gentle and quiet; a true gentleman in every sense. But he always knew when he was right and when he was right there was no argument. End of debate – he was right.'

Telling *Billboard* about what had attracted his multi-platinum ears to the studio for album after album, Fairbairn explained, 'Little Mountain isn't a first-flight studio compared to some others. It hasn't got the best gear and it's certainly not a fancy place. But it does have a unique sound to it that only four or five people in the world can capture ...

There's a certain, unpretentious feeling there, a certain something you can't define, that is conducive to making great rock records.'

Fairbairn's manager, Sandee Bathgate, who booked Fairbairn and AC/DC into the studio in 1990, added of the studio's magic atmosphere that 'basically any studio is four walls and a tape machine. It's the chemistry that happens between a band and producer and their engineer.' Offering an additional compliment to engineer Mike Fraser, Bathgate said, 'Little Mountain has to be commended for hiring exceptional assistants. When you're working with the likes of Fairbairn, you'll learn through osmosis alone.'

Of the sonic strengths that Fairbairn brought to the console, engineer Mike Fraser recalled, 'In one way they [AC/DC] are a tough band to produce because they already know what they want and how to get it. They just need that third member of the band, so to speak, to help guide them to those ends. In the dynamic between Bruce and the band, they liked his approach in general. Bruce is a take-charge kind of guy, and so he was the perfect guy for them. He was a great producer, first, because he had a good musical background – he was a horn player and understood music – and, while you don't usually have to read music doing the rock thing, he could understand and read that stuff. One of his greatest qualities is he was sort of like a coach, and could come in and play referee – if some of the band members were having a disagreement, he could get all of that smoothed out.

'Second, he always had an agenda, so every day he'd walk in and say, "OK, at noon, we're going to record a guitar part, at 2:35 we're gonna do this," so he'd have the day laid out and wouldn't let it get out of hand. Because sometimes musicians, when everybody gets creative and are working out a guitar part, can get a little micro-focused. Bruce would give them a couple tries, and then say, "OK, nope – that needs to be developed more. You need to go home and work that out, and we'll move on to something else and record you tomorrow." So he never allowed too much time to be wasted in the studio, was always very efficient, and with that approach you tend overall to get a lot of great stuff done, because you don't get bogged down on exploring something out. You just come in and capture the magic.'

That magic, Fraser recalled, was captured 'on an SSL 4000 console in Studio B, which is a fairly small room'.

The band had the advantage of having already completed songwriting for the record, courtesy of Malcolm and Angus. The brothers had taken the creative helm – including penning the lyrics – due to what Angus described as the distraction on Brian Johnson's part of a divorce. 'Mal and I thought it would ease the pressure on him if we wrote the words,' he told rock journalist Paul Stenning. 'We've always contributed in the past anyway. We'd sit down, the three of us – me, Mal and

Bon – sometimes four of us with my brother George, and we'd have this big shoot around. We always gave Bon a helping hand in the past; same with Brian, because if you have some lyrical idea while you're writing it can save you a lot of heartache and trouble at the end of the day.'

Indeed, after dealing with the stresses and pressures the divorce put on his collective energies, the vocalist himself told Stenning, 'I just ran out of ideas. I just can't think of enough. I don't want to write the same thing again. And Angus and Malcolm helped Bon with a lot of the lyrics in the earlier days. Mal and Ang have this songwriting in their blood – they are very good at it. They just let go. I just felt terrible when we were doing an idea – I didn't have much ideas-wise. I thought I'd wait to see the boys and hear them playing the riffs. I was having a real tough time thinking up lyrics. That just happens sometimes: you just dry up. Well, the boys said, "We'll give it a try," and the boys gave it a thought, and it was great. It was from a different angle.'

'And Angus has the craziest ideas. Angus is way out there – he comes back, gets these crazy things in his head and they are great. Angus and Malcolm are just that talented. But what I still do, and what I love very much, is to meet Malcolm and Angus in London. They'll say, "Come on, Brian, we have a few ideas." And that's the best part of it, because I know I will be the first person in the world to hear them. And I help them to shape the songs. We just sit down there, and it's lovely. You're with your pals, drinking lots of coffee – I just love it.'

Against that backdrop, Angus felt the band had plenty of time for pre-production in planning what would unofficially be considered their comeback album. In contrast to past albums, he told Stenning, 'we had plenty of time, which was good. In the past we've always been committed to something. Sometimes we've even been committed to touring, with the dates set and we wouldn't even be finished with the record. This time, there was no pressure on us, which was great. We could write songs, take some time and listen to them, and say, "That's good," or "That needs help." Maybe change a piece here or there. We don't really like to go into the studio with nothing and try to do it there. We like to have it done and worked out, so that when you're recording you can concentrate on the performance and the sound.'

In an interview with journalist Martin Aston, Angus added that, with *The Razors Edge*, 'instead of being riffmakers all the time and thinking we could make tunes out of them, we started from the other end of the scale and concentrated on coming up with full songs ... You always make the best album you can for that period. We never have, never would, put something out unless we felt confident about it. This time, we kept pushing the deadline for completion further and further back so that the record was right.'

That said, once inside the studio, Brian Johnson told *Juke* there was a much more focused environment. 'Malcolm and Angus are real workaholics. As long as you pull your weight, you're OK. Once you become a lightweight, you suffer their wrath.'

Offering fans a peek into the brothers' writing process, Malcolm told rock journalist Murray Engleheart that he and Angus worked well together because 'we can bounce off each other – that's the good side of it. And guitar-wise, we know each other. We've been playing together longer than AC/DC has been around, as far as knowing what each other does and how to play guitar with each other. That's the thing that's just evolved from being brothers. At the other end of it, basically when we're out on the road and recording, we're working together as well as being brothers, so it's a typical brotherly relationship, I guess. We know the band's bigger than anything. We always call musical differences small because nothing's worth ending everything over. So we'll never bother; we'll get over it quick if we have it out or whatever. When it happens, we usually know we'll sort it out. After 20 years, I think you've got to do that.'

Though Malcolm and Angus brought in the album's songs largely written, Brian recalled one experience that 'reminded me of the old days when we would experiment with the arrangements and just try things out for the fun of it. In the back of our minds we realised that there is a whole generation of fans that has sprung up in the three years since our last album was released. I want them to see what all this noise and fun is all about.'

One aspect of their recording process that the band kept unchanged – as newly installed drummer Chris Slade recalled to journalist Stenning – was tracking live off the floor. 'It's inconceivable, say, for Angus to stop by [at the studio] two weeks after the rest of the band to record his guitar parts. And they always keep the first takes. On every track of every AC/DC album, there's always some element of a first take somewhere.'

Engineer Mike Fraser recalled that the setup at Studio B at Little Mountain was ideal for tracking the band live off the floor because it didn't have a doorway into the loading bay. 'So you had more of the small room sound, which works with AC/DC, because they like the tighter, closer-sounding drums. The drum miking setup, on the snare drum, was [to] mike the top and bottom with a Shure 57, and on the kick would be a Sennheiser 421, and on the toms, I again used a Shure 57 on the top skin, and on the bottom, miked it up with a Sennheiser 421 as well.

'I like the Sennheiser because it's got a really good sort of attack quality to it, and I use the Shure mics because they can take a lot of abuse and you can even hit them with a drumstick and they'll keep on working. The only difference in the mic I use for maybe a real heavy hitter is maybe not mike the drums as close, to get a little more distance on it. Because, when you hit a drum really hard, the sound jumps up so fast that it sounds like a smack, so you've got to catch that sound wave a little further away from the instrument, because that's where the tone comes back in.'

While listeners might have expected new drummer Chris Slade to be as heavy a hitter as he looked on video or on TV, Fraser recalled that recording him in the studio was funny 'because Chris is actually quite a light drummer – he doesn't hit very hard. When you watch him on videos, it looks like he's really laying into them, but, in the studio, when he hits the cymbals they barely move. That's sort of the clue, and some of those drummers who hit with a little bit more finesse, it's actually an easier sound to record, because the drum skins react a little better. They don't shut down with the force going on. So especially on overheads, I'd mike him a little closer because he doesn't put all his weight into it – he's more of a finesse guy. The overheads I used on Chris were probably AKG 452s – they don't get too thin. It's still warm, but has a nice silky top-end – that's why I like those.'

Angus told Stenning why he felt Chris Slade was an ideal drummer for the group's sound: 'His style is just perfect for the band – it is as solid and powerful as you can get. Chris is a bit similar to Phil Rudd – they both smash the drums as hard as they can. But Chris can be frightening to look at – you look at his bald head and it could scare you.'

When attention turned to tracking guitars, Fraser said that 'on *Razor's Edge*, it was a little different from later records I made with them, because the songs were already recorded, so we were just doing overdubs. So on that one they didn't play at the same time. We set up the amp heads in the control room, and Angus would sit there with a cigarette hanging out of his mouth and play. I miked him up with 57s on his Marshalls, not much of a room sound on them, because both he and Malcolm like a little bit tighter, close-miked type of sound.'

'Angus, as a lead player, has just this great, singular knack for coming up with stuff in the spur of the moment. Again, when we were doing *Razor's Edge*, we were doing his solos, and I remember he'd done a pass on one song. I said, "Hey, that's great – let's just do another one just to have an alternate," and he played a completely different solo. Then we did a third one and it was an *entirely different* solo, and they were all three competitively great. So now it was like: "Great – how do we choose between these?!"'

When they got to the album's lead single, 'Thunderstruck', Angus recalled of its creation to Stenning that – as with many of music's most inspired moments – 'I was just fiddling around with my left hand when I came up with that riff. I played it more by accident than anything. I thought, "Not bad" and put it on tape. That's how me and Malcolm generally work. We put our ideas on tape and play them for each other.'

'[The lyrical concept came to me while] I was in an airplane over East Germany and the plane got struck by lightning. I thought my number was up. The stewardess said we were struck by lightning and I said, "No, we were struck by thunder, because it boomed."'

When it came time to track what would become the band's biggest international hit in almost a decade, Fraser recalled that 'on "Thunderstruck", that was so cool, because Angus said, "Well, we have this little intro thing," and whipped out that little opening part, and it was only going to be on the intro. So, as we start recording, Angus goes through the intro, and then, as the first verse came up, he was still playing and Bruce went, "OK, let him roll, and see where it goes." He wound up continuing to play it throughout the whole song in one take! By the end, he had this big long ash of a cigarette hanging out of his mouth, that he'd smoked throughout that one take.

'If you listen to the finished song, you can notice in the mix we faded it in and out, so it sort of disappears a little bit in the verses and choruses, and comes in and out, but it's played top to bottom, all the way through, one pass – it was awesome!'

For the album's title track, Angus told Stenning that 'we had the main riff and there was something really ominous about it. And for that reason alone we decided to go ahead with it. In the past we'd stay away from things that sounded too musical.'

As attentions turned to the album's vocals, the band kept the same musical principle in mind, with Brian adding that 'there's a lot more melody on *The Razors Edge* and we've always been wary of melody. A song like 'Moneytalks' or 'Thunderstruck' – there are real melodies in those songs. I had to learn what to do again with that.'

For what *Brave Words / Bloody Knuckles* hailed as 'possibly the greatest live show opener ever – period', Fraser focused on the song's sing-a-long backing vocals. 'We had Brian all sung and the main vocal comp done,' he recalled, 'and for the big gang "Thunder" vocal, that was Angus, Malcolm and Cliff. We never get Brian in there for backing vocals because his voice is so distinct that, if you add him to the backgrounds, it will kind of take over. With any harmony-type parts, it's usually Cliff who does all those.

'We use an 87 or 414 for the backgrounds, because you don't want to load up all similar sounds on the vocals – you want a little bit of variety. So, for instance, because the 58 mic has its own characteristics, if you did all your backgrounds with that, it would start clouding in the way of the lead vocal.'

For Brian's lead vocals, Fraser added that 'the vocal mic I like using best, especially with singers like Brian Johnson, is a Shure 58. They just use it as a hand-held, as they would live on stage. It handles the force of their voice, and has a great sound to it that's nice and crisp but still has body. I find with guys like that, if you use a really nice tube mic, say, it doesn't really handle their force or sibilance as well as a 58 will do.'

When the band tracked 'Moneytalks' – a massive hit single that *Kerrang!* hailed years later as a song that still took 'the piss out of 99 per cent of rock bands' – Fraser singled it out as one of those lightning-in-the-bottle moments of studio magic. 'I remember it all coming together really fast. They're a really fast band in the studio – even if they're not rehearsed, they're such a great band at what they do after playing together all these years. So they come in, and there will be a quick bass, drums two-guitar set-up and away we would go, and after a couple hours, there's the song.'

Discussing the song's lyrical focus, Angus explained to Stenning that the words were the band's attempt to convey the idea that 'money's the big divider. Places other than America are not necessarily like that. In Europe, they think you've got to be born with class. In the US, they think you buy it, it comes with the tux. So it's just our little dig at the lifestyle of the rich and the faceless.'

Angus recalled to journalist Aston that, when recording wrapped and the band turned to choosing the album's title, 'we wanted a title that sounded tough, to cut the bullshit … Because that's what we are, in our music, though not as people. We aren't Mike Tysons! But the music we're playing comes in for a lot of fire – not from the public, but it's never been the media's most favourite music.'

But in this case, it would be. As the band debuted at No. 2 on the Top 200 Album Chart, *Billboard* celebrated the album's embodying the 'quintessential AC/DC – rowdy, abrasive, unapologetically fun metal full of blistering power chords, memorable hooks, and testosterone-driven lyrics'. *Blender* magazine's later overview would declare that, with *Razors Edge*, 'AC/DC reclaimed the old spirit on their first album of the '90s', and even the typically conservative *National Review* were won over enough to declare that 'the Johnson years are best represented by 1990's *The Razors Edge*'.

The album's crown jewel with fans and critics alike – 'Thunderstruck' – was the sort of hard rock that everyone felt AC/DC excelled at, with *Blender* hailing it 'as anthemic as anything from Scott's golden age'. *Entertainment Weekly* best summed up the achievement of song and album – which went on to sell five million copies – with their observation that 'AC/DC explodes on its new album's first track "Thunderstruck" with enough coiled fury to make you think it invented the genre'.

CHAPTER TWELVE

BALLBREAKER (1995)

'It was pure magic again, you know? We'd become so
self-indulgent and just had to get pure
AC/DC back. I think, once we really thought about it,
we thought if we're going to do this right we should
look at Phil [Rudd] ... Probably it's
a bit late but it seems the right time now!'
MALCOLM YOUNG

Producer Rick Rubin came to AC/DC's 1995 studio LP, *Ballbreaker*, as a lifelong fan. 'Most of the kids in my high school were into bands like Led Zeppelin, Yes and Pink Floyd, and I spent a lot of time hating those bands,' he told *Rolling Stone*. 'Two bands grabbed me, Aerosmith and AC/DC. 'DC were kicking with that great huge guitar. I remember being impressed by all the things they tell you are wrong – volume, power, the simple riffs. And Bon Scott was just brilliant.

'I'll go on the record as saying they're the greatest rock 'n' roll band of all time. They didn't write emotional lyrics. They didn't play emotional songs. The emotion is all in that groove. And that groove is timeless.'

BALLBREAKER (1995)

It was in that spirit that the band chose Rubin to produce their 13th studio album. As returning drummer Phil Rudd explained to rock journalist Paul Stenning, 'One of the reasons we used Rick Rubin was to recreate the feeling of the earlier albums. We wanted to get that classic AC/DC sound back, the sound that suits us best.'

Recounting how the band had reached out to him about rejoining the fold, Rudd quipped to *Musician* magazine, 'I was trying to find a pen when Malcolm called. I was absolutely gobsmacked. I had seen them with another drummer [Chris Slade] who was doing a good job, so I never expected that they would have the need to call me again. But Malcolm and I were out having a beer and I'd joked, "Any time, Mal." I hadn't seen him for eight years when they phoned up and wanted me to come to the show. There were no hard feelings… It is just sort of a groove thing. I didn't really think about it too much. We have a good thing – there is a natural interplay between us that we are very conscious of and we enjoy, but without thinking about it. It is just what it is.'

'He seemed just like the old Phil,' Malcolm recalled to *Mojo* of the drummer's return. 'When we started on the album, me and Angus said, "Let's bring him down and have a jam and see how it goes," and it was just like the old days.

'We always seem to know when we've had enough of a break,' he added to Stenning. 'Though it wasn't as long a break as some people think. We got together and jammed and the songs seemed to just fall into place.'

It was an offer Phil couldn't refuse, and he joined the mutual admiration society in an interview with *Modern Drummer*. 'I always fired up best when I was playing with these guys, so I really couldn't see how I wasn't going to do it.'

Bassist Cliff Williams echoed the celebratory attitude, declaring excitedly to *Guitar World*, 'Phil's back! He was the band's original drummer, but needed to step out for a number of years for various reasons. Now he's back with a vengeance and we're working very well with him. It's great to have him back – he's always been the right man for the job.'

Angus concurred, saying to *Guitar* magazine that '[Phil is] the one who set the drumming style of the band.'

As a fan both of the band and of the drummer, Rick Rubin too was delighted. In an interview with *Rhythm* magazine, he said, 'The best thing was the return of Phil Rudd, who had left the band in 1982. To me, that made them AC/DC again … The thing that separates AC/DC as a hard-rock band is that you can dance to their music. They didn't play funk, but everything they played was funky. And that beat could really get a crowd going … You can hear it in how he drags behind the beat. It's that same rhythm that first drew me to them in junior high.'

Sadly, the odd man out was the unfortunate Chris Slade,

who said that, following his dismissal, 'I was so disgusted I didn't touch my drum kit for three years.'

When the band met up with Rubin to present some of what they'd been writing in pre-production, Angus recalled to Stenning, 'My first impression was this big guy, twice my height, with sunglasses, lying on the floor doing yoga and telling us what a big AC/DC fan he was.'

Malcolm added that 'he said he'd been an AC/DC fan since he was a kid in New York, and "Highway To Hell" was one of the first tracks he'd ever done with a rap group.'

From bassist Cliff Williams's perspective, the fact that Rubin was younger than the band was an advantage for them. 'It's good to have young blood,' he told *Guitar World*. 'Rick's loved the band for years – at least that's what he says – and wanted to work with us some more. He knew that the band has its own sound and knew what we wanted to hear. He doesn't try to get us to do things that don't suit us.'

In the interests of continuity, AC/DC again enlisted engineer Mike Fraser to work alongside Rubin. Fraser felt he'd been rehired because 'Right from the get-go, from when we'd done *Razors Edge*, the band had really liked the guitar sounds I helped get. And because I've been an AC/DC fan right from the very beginning, I also sort of "got" their sound, and as a fan appreciated it, and could help them get it and retain it. I understand that sound, unlike other engineers who go in and start putting reverb on the drums and making Angus play through a delay pedal or something – that's not who they are.'

'So because I get their sound and understand completely what they're like, they like that comfort level, and no matter who's producing them, they know I'm watching their back as well. I've been fortunate over the last two decades for the band to have requested me to be in on making their records, and that was the situation heading into their collaboration with Rick.'

No matter what the musical soundscape might be, Rick Rubin's production style is to be methodical – so much so that, heading into the recording of *Ballbreaker*, the band spent 10 weeks in New York tracking roughly 50 hours of demos. 'Rick Rubin made us record every track about 50 times each to obtain the good dynamics and we kept those who got the best feelings,' Cliff Williams told *Rhythm*. 'We wanted to do a good album ... and that's what we did.' But it wasn't all plain sailing, Cliff recalled. 'The making of the album was really hard ... We started to record at the Record Plant Studios, in New York, but we didn't enjoy the sound we had. Many musicians told us, "It's an excellent studio to record drums parts." But we tried the drums in each of the rooms of those studios and [couldn't get] a decent sound. We fixed carpets on the walls, and we put a tent on to the kit too, to obtain a more live sound. Result: we lose two months by turning around. The only positive thing is that we knew perfectly every new song.'

BALLBREAKER (1995)

From the drummer's own perspective, Phil recalled in an interview with *Rhythm* that 'when we started doing *Ballbreaker* there was a bit of a difference of opinion in the studio about drum sounds and we were working with a new producer. So we went through this big rigmarole where we couldn't play together because of the sound reflecting off the wall. It was bizarre! ... We tried playing on risers and even had a marquee built over the riser to contain the room sound. This was before we got started.'

'Then they brought in a "drum doctor" from Europe and he had cases full of bass drums and snare drums, but at the end of the day we sent him packing because I knew that the problem wasn't down to the sound of my gear. It's a very personal thing and I always do things the best way. That's how it is. In the end we went to another studio.'

Adding technical commentary on the band's decision to relocate to Ocean Way in Los Angeles, Fraser recalled that 'where we started — a studio in New York at the Power Station — which is this big, giant ambient room, which is not the band's sound at all. They just wanted a really close sound — especially on that record — so we spent four or five weeks in New York trying to get the right drum sound. We even hired a circus tent, put burlap sacks on all the walls trying to deaden things down, and nothing was working. So we ended up moving to a studio in LA and finished up there.'

Once the band had relocated to LA, Malcolm told rock

journalist Murray Engleheart that they took a couple of weeks' breathing space and found a recording studio, Ocean Way. 'After we started working in LA, the sounds were just a little bit more real … So we virtually started again and re-recorded three or four of the tracks we thought we already had. So we basically just did a whole re-start.'

Fortunately, the band was well rehearsed because of the regimen that had preceded entering Ocean Way. Malcolm explained to journalist Stenning that this had involved jamming a lot and 'because of the delays in the studio, we jammed even more! I'd say we were together almost a year just playing, making this album. Things got really tight, the sort of thing you usually only get on tour. So that gave us a great vibe in the studio. We want our albums to sound like our best live gigs, and normally you have to shut your eyes and imagine you're back onstage again. But this time we were already in the stage mode.'

Ocean Way studio is almost as legendary as the band itself. Its fame springs from its founder and chief designer, Bill Putnam, considered by many within the industry to be the father of modern recording. According to Ocean Way's website, 'Putnam is acknowledged to be the first person to use artificial reverberation for commercial recording. He also developed the first multi-band equalisers, and with his company Universal Audio, was responsible for the development of classic equipment like the Urei 1176LN and Urei Time Align

Monitors. He was involved in the early development of stereophonic recording and founded studios in Chicago, Hollywood and San Francisco.'

'The Los Angeles-based Ocean Way Studios, born out of a partnership in the late 1970s between Putnam and Allen Sides, led by the early 1980s to Allen buying close to a thousand tube microphones from overseas. The European studios and broadcasters were dumping loads of "antiquated" tube mics for brand-new phantom-powered transistor mics. He carefully went through every mic, picking the absolutely best of the best and selling off the rest. This is how, along with the mics from the previous studio buyouts, Ocean Way amassed one of the largest collection of tube mics in the world.'

'By 1988, Allen was beginning to run out of space and luckily was able to purchase Record One Recording ... [He] moved in quickly, re-did the monitor systems to be more compatible with Ocean Way, and opened for business with two studios that contained very nice custom API consoles. Soon after that, Allen constructed the largest (112 inputs with GML automation) totally discrete Neve console in the world. Ocean Way now had seven rooms operating in LA, headquartered at 6000 Sunset Blvd.'

By the early 1990s, Ocean Way had become the go-to studio in LA for top producers such as Rick Rubin and Don Was (Rolling Stones, Bob Dylan, Iggy Pop, The Black

Crowes, Willie Nelson, Stone Temple Pilots and many more). Was explained to *Billboard* why he thought Ocean Way remained such an attraction in a more modern age: 'When I was a kid and looked at photos of sessions, studios looked like Ocean Way … They probably *were* pictures from Ocean Way, but, when I was finally old enough to do the gig I'd dreamed of as a kid, everyone else had remodelled in some asinine quest to remain modern. They'd wiped out the very thing that made them great. [Ocean Way] had the good sense never to touch the walls. It felt like you were in a real studio – you felt connected to music history.'

Warner Bros. Records senior staff producer Rob Cavallo (Green Day, Alanis Morissette, Kid Rock, Dave Matthews Band, Meat Loaf) added of the studio's lure that its new owner Allen Sides had carried on Putnam's tradition of understanding 'the essentials of what producers and artists needs. That "big picture" stuff, like truly great-sounding monitors, truly functioning boards. The maintenance is fantastic: everything sounds like it is supposed to sound. It's his personal vibe as well. He understands what we're going for when we go into a studio, and he supplies it so well and in such a comfortable manner.'

In its cover story on the studio's 25th anniversary in the 1990s, *Billboard* declared that these producers' analysis of Ocean Way's multi-room recording, mix and mastering facility 'is shared by innumerable audio professionals'. AC/DC's collaboration with Rubin would add to that legacy.

No matter that the band was plugging in to record together for the first time since 1990: Angus told *Hit Parader* that, once the tape was rolling in Studio D, the band played as if no time at all had passed. 'When we get together and go to work, something special always happens. It doesn't matter how long we may have been apart – once we're all in the same place at the same time, we become AC/DC.'

Malcolm described AC/DC's goal for the album as their desire 'to get back to the old feel of the rhythm. The feel dominated this time. And really, the best feels are the simplest parts.'

Despite breaking their own rule in opting to write many of the album's songs at the studio, Brian Johnson recalled of these sessions that, 'We were having such a good time I didn't want to go home! When we all first got together it's always fun, because you haven't got a clue what is going to happen next. The boys just come in with some riffs – and I don't know where they get them from, they're brilliant. And all I have to do is open my mouth and shout my tits off!'

The band tracked live off the floor as usual, with bassist Cliff Williams telling *Rhythm* magazine that they wouldn't have it any other way. 'We've always recorded live, playing all four of us, together. As time has gone by, we tried to record with a click but, with Phil, it's totally useless. We record basic tracks – tracks' bones – then Angus adds his guitar parts. For *Ballbreaker*, we put every speaker in different rooms. Malcolm, Angus and me played in a small room with glass partitions, to enable ourselves to see Phil, who was still in the main room.'

AC/DC's fansite crabsodyinblue.com gives a detailed insight into what the band used in these recording sessions. 'To record the *Ballbreaker* album Angus Young used three Gibson SG guitars. The primary guitar he used was a 1964 model and he used Ernie Ball regular-gauge strings – .010 but with a .048 on the lower E. For solos he used a 1968 model strung with Ernie Ball Super Slinkys. For power chords he used another 1968 model with Super Slinkys. Malcolm Young used the same 1963 Gretsch Jet Firebird he has used since the start of AC/DC, although the guitar has been altered through the years. For strings he used .012 to .056 Gibson strings with a wound G (.025). Cliff Williams used a 1976 Music Man bass strung with Leavy O'Addarno flatwounds. For amps Malcolm used 100 watt Marshall heads and Angus used one 4x12 and a JTM-4s head Marshall. The main technicians for the album were Alan Rogan and Rick St Pierre.'

Phil Rudd, meanwhile, used his favourite Sonor Signature series. 'I'm always looking for a fat, intimidating sound that's punchy with an edge on it, so I can hear everything cutting through,' he explained to *Rhythm*. 'Sonor drums are built very strongly and they're the only kit I could really use, to be honest. I've seen a lot of other kits, and nobody builds 'em better than Sonor. I've still got my Signature series kit, which I had built over 20 years ago, and some of the hardware is still like brand new. The chrome doesn't have a mark on it and just doesn't chip. But they're a helluva weight to drag around.'

In drawing a contrast between tracking Phil and former drummer Chris Slade, engineer Fraser began by explaining that they are quite different drummers. 'Chris has a lot of finesse and a light touch, whereas Phil is a thumper and a basher, so it's sometimes hard to record and capture his thing just because he's so bombastic. It's like riding a bull – you have to be ready for it. We change snare heads in between every take just because they get so beat up, he's just a fantastic hitter!'

One thing Fraser did feel the two drummers had in common was that 'once they'd had their drum parts done, they'd go home, and don't stay for the whole recording of the album.'

With Phil, bassist Cliff Williams felt like they were picking right up where they'd left off a decade earlier. 'Phil is really the groove,' he told *Rhythm*. 'His play is simple, like mine, still being strong and fixable. Chris Slade was more a technician, kind of a "studio shark". Simon [Wright] knew every song! His play was too simple too, but he wasn't Phil Rudd. Phil's play is exactly what we need.'

'Moreover, he's got this sixth sense. Phil's always had a natural feel for what the band was about. Chris is a fantastic drummer but Phil fits us like a hand in a glove. So it's nothing specific, more of a feeling. He was in the band even before I joined and when I came in the group already ran like a well-oiled machine. I had to fit in with it and that's what I did.'

Describing the back-to-basics spirit of the sessions, Angus explained to *Guitar Player*, 'When we made *Ballbreaker*, the plan was we wanted to do a stripped-down record, a bit hard and tough. Yet again, I think what was being played [on the radio at the time] was dance things, mostly the disco-type dance. We felt we should get in and do a nice tough rock record, maybe a bit more hard-edged. You can hear it on the "Ballbreaker" track, you can hear it on "Hail Caesar" and especially "Hard as a Rock".'

Engineer Mike Fraser painted a broader picture by describing Rubin's production style as equally 'bare bones'. 'Rick is a fairly hands-off type of producer. He leaves the band to kind of do their own thing, then will come in later on that night, listen to what they've done, make some suggestions, then repeat the whole process the next day.'

Brian Johnson confirmed this practise-till-perfect process to *Mojo*. 'He would come in at night and say, "Hmm, we'll try that song a different way tomorrow."'

This didn't always go down too well at the time and affected the band's impression of the progress they were making as the weeks went on. Cliff Williams explained to *Rhythm*, 'Rick Rubin made us record every track about 50 times each to obtain the good dynamics, and we kept those tracks that had the best feelings. Sometimes, when we heard the whole tracks, our opinion changed totally. It was a bit disappointing and I thought we'd lose the sacred fire by playing all those tracks again and again.'

Brian Johnson agreed, quipping, 'By the time we finished, we'd played the song so many different times you'd be sitting there going, "Jesus, I'm sick of this bloody thing."'

Mike Fraser, the man who sat through those 50 times day in day out, recalled, 'When we recorded this album, [digital platform] Pro Tools was just coming on the market. We were recording analogue, which might have been a pain in the ass with other bands, but AC/DC is just awesome because they do a first take of something and say, "Wow, that was pretty good, although it kind of sped up a bit in the chorus – let's try a second take." The second take would be great, and the third take would be even better, but you could tell they'd peaked on the third take, so we'd keep that one.'

'It's always live, one take through. The only time we replace anything is if there's one guitar chord that's out of tune – we'll punch in for that. But with them, there's virtually no editing at all – they just keep going live.'

The band seemed particularly appreciative of engineer Mike Fraser's constant console companionship. Indeed, Malcolm hailed him as 'indispensable' in the album's recording, so much so that he was given a production credit on it. 'Because Rick was fairly hands-off,' Fraser explained, 'and because I was in there in the trenches day in and out, at the end of the record the band said, "OK, we're going to give you a production credit." But I wouldn't really say I was a producer on that record. I was more an engineer, but, because of my added role in helping them make that record, they opted generously to give me a production credit.'

In miking guitarists Malcolm, Angus and Cliff, the engineer recalled that 'with the bass, Cliff plays into an SVT bass amp with a Phet 47 mic on that, plus I'll usually throw a 57 up to kind of get a barky, kind of cone-sound from the speaker. Cliff's really simple, just get some bottom end going on him, and make sure it works well with the thump of the kick drum, and away we go.'

Angus tracked solos on his trusty Gibson SG, as he told *Guitar Player*, 'I just use the SGs. I would say my favourite one is from about '67 or '68. It used to have one of those engraved metal things on the back [base plate] with the little arm – the tremolo – but I replaced that with another tailpiece. But I've got a couple of them that have the vibrato arm still … When I bought the first one – and I've still got it now – it was like a gift. It was something I always wanted. I went into this shop and picked it up, and it was so easy for me to play. I always thought that it was just a run-of-the-mill

Gibson, that they were all basically like that, and that you might get better ones. Over the years, I've never found one that was the same as it ... I have maybe 16 or 17 now.'

Offering some insight into the band's writing on the album, Angus explained to Engleheart that – as with every past AC/DC album – his principle for writing riffs was vested squarely in a musical moral he'd heard many years ago. '[There] was a guy doing a thing about Chuck Berry and he thought, "Oh, Chuck Berry, he's so straightahead – it's the same licks." But when he listened, he found each time it was different and then, when he started really getting into it, he started to see other pieces of the puzzle. Because in Chuck there's jazz, there's country, there's the blues element and there's that rock 'n' roll. Then the great thing is he always knew when to play and when not to, and he'd pull it back.'

Talking to journalist Susan Masino about the creation of some of the individual album tracks, Malcolm said, 'The title track was the last song we wrote and it came together real quick. We just thought of the hardest and heaviest thing we could, and it came from there and just seemed to sum the whole thing up.'

When attention turned to the vocals, it was again a group affair as Brian Johnson described to Masino. 'We did all the vocals right in the control room, just sitting around like we're sitting here now. Malcolm was sitting on one side of me with Mike Fraser on the other, because I don't like going into the booth to sing. I like it to be more like when I'm onstage with the others, to have them around me like that.'

'We always track Brian in the control room rather than setting him up out in the main room,' Mike Fraser confirmed. 'So we're always sitting there side by side. He's very easygoing, likes a little bit of tea now and then, and likes to have an ash tray by his side because he smokes while he sings. Brian sings fairly dry, maybe with just a quick slap delay on his vocal just to kind of get some vibe going, but it's usually pretty dry – we don't use reverb or anything. Again, with that band, they like a more sort of upfront, punchy kind of sound anyway.'

In outlining some of the technical challenges that came with Brian's singular brand of hard-rock belting, Fraser began by explaining, 'Brian is not vocally trained, so he kind of scrunches his throat down and creates this rasp in there. I don't know how he's still got a throat to do it, but what comes out is awesome. In saying that, sometimes Brian's a little bit of work in the studio because it takes so much energy to sing the way he sings. So just to keep that full quality and nice grit to his voice – it wears down fast and he might start getting a little bit hoarse – you can't sing him too long, maybe an hour to an hour-and-a-half a day. Then he's got to rest till later on that night or the next day.'

When Brian was recording, Fraser added, '[the] vocals on the Rubin record were mostly Brian and I. If there was any questions about a certain part and the way it would be sung, we'd refer to Angus and Malcolm, so Rick was quite hands-off on that.'

Upon release, the band's back-to-basics move paid off with both hard-rock purists and younger grunge fans, who'd grown up in one generation or another of AC/DC's straight-up, power-chord rock 'n' roll. Critics were dazzled by an album *Rolling Stone* described as 'tighter and slightly cleaner sounding than the group's last studio album ... The boys seem to be going for a bluesier feel.'

The band was clearly enthusiastic about the results of their half-year studio experiment. 'I'm really proud of this album,' Angus told journalist Stenning. 'I can honestly say I love every one of the songs – and that's saying something, coming from a band that started just before the crucifixion!'

Phil Rudd told the same writer that on listening back to his first creative collaboration with the band in over a decade, 'I'm really pleased with the results. I had the most fun I've ever had in a studio with this one.'

Rubin himself would add in an interview that, for him, ultimately the album was 'a tribute to how great they were'.

Ballbreaker debuted at No. 4 on the Billboard Top 200 Album Chart, spawning the hits 'Hard as a Rock' and 'Hail Caesar' and going on to sell two million copies. AC/DC had triumphed on a new level that few other hard-rock bands – aside from their main competitor and biggest fans Aerosmith – had achieved in making their own particular rock genre a mainstream mainstay. AC/DC's hard-rock blueprint had held up as reliably as any other band, and in the arena of rock 'n' roll, as MTV eloquently concluded, 'they deliver guilty-pleasure metal like no other hard-rock band'.

In 1998, Brian expanded his artistic side projects into the realm of record production, throwing an unknown band – Florida rockers Neurotica – the chance of the lifetime. The story, as recounted by the band's website, went like this: 'A local band with good following plays a dive in their hometown and a great set of ears happens to be in the audience. No, not the ears of some A&R rep obliged to attend a gig to cover a week in the sun at the expense of a label, but the knowing ears of AC/DC lead singer, Brian Johnson! The famous rocker loves the band, buys them beers and the next thing you know there's an album being made with Johnson at the production helm and one of the rock world's top engineers, Mike Fraser, mixing. The result: Neurotica's debut release: *Seed*.' He produced a second album for them a year later

CHAPTER THIRTEEN

STIFF UPPER LIP (2000)

'This one was a 135,000-cigarette album.
I can always tell if we're making a good one when the
smokes are going before, during and after a take'
BRIAN JOHNSON

With the arrival of 2000's *Stiff Upper Lip* on 28 February 2000, the critical consensus was 'Hey, they did it again.' And, in the context of consistency, they very much had. While the band's 14th studio LP covered no new ground, it didn't give up any of the sonic fundamentals that had made AC/DC's hard rock the genre's signature for the previous quarter century. As *NME* pointed out in its review, 'their 17th album, business as usual, no ballsing about it ... A band with a sound as pure as science ... they're immovable. Every song is like architecture ... it is we, listening to the stunning simplicity of *Stiff Upper Lip*, who are moved to wonder why on earth anyone would be daft enough to aim for anything else.'

Again the band returned to their production home base

with big brother George. Angus told *Mojo* that a return to the studio with George felt like a logical reunion for the band. 'He helped us when we were doing the *Bonfire* box set, and from that we thought it would be great to work with him again. He had actually stopped producing for the past five years and taken a back seat, but even when we worked with other people we always liked him to hear everything before it was released. Being his younger brothers, I suppose we still look to him even now for his stamp of approval.

'I always think we did the great rock tunes when we worked with my brother George. The whole thing is not to get too serious and hung up about things. It's about having fun and a good time.'

Describing the sonic direction the band was seeking this time around, engineer Mike Fraser recalled that 'the band specifically came in saying, "We want a really dry, bluesy-type record." They didn't want that ballsy-riff rock sound. So the way AC/DC comes in to record, they're doing it for their own enjoyment, rather than being motivated by trends. *Stiff Upper Lip* was a bit of a departure from where they've usually gone, and my job as their engineer is always to capture what they want, and on that record, they definitely conveyed to me that they wanted a drier, little bit warmer-sounding album.'

'Bluesy' and 'drier' translated, according to Angus in an interview with rock journalist Murray Engleheart, into 'just two guitars and your bass and drums, and really the only

Above: Drummer Chris Slade in his Manfred Mann incarnation.

© *Rex Features*

Below: AC/DC doing it al fresco in 1975.

© *Rex Features*

Legendary producer Rick Rubin.   © *Rex Features*

Above: Simon Wright and Brian Johnson in the early 1980s.   © *Getty Images*

Below: A band press conference.   © *Rex Features*

Another AC/DC production talent, Mutt Lange, with former wife, country singer Shania Twain.

Cliff Williams in full voice.

Above: The brothers Young at the mixing desk.   © *Getty Images*

Below: AC/DC were inducted into the Rock'n'Roll Hall of Fame by Aerosmith's Steven Tyler in 2003.   © *Rex Features*

Performing at Wembley with the rotating statue of Angus behind Brian Johnson and Angus Young.

© Rex Features

colour they use is me for a bit of the guitar work. You try to keep everything minimalist, I suppose, if you're thinking in an art way – you keep it basic. The good rock 'n' roll bands are always the bare bones stuff. I always think the best rock out there is stuff that has got the blues element in it. They're sort of bombarding us these days with image, and that seems to be more and more the case. I think they're all sort of losing track.'

Engineer Mike Fraser added in an interview with *Sound on Sound* magazine that the fact that each producer had a slightly different working method was of little consequence. 'The band play the way they play, and they know what they're doing, so there's not a lot of coaching to be done.'

For Fraser, the band's choice of direction meant a slight adjustment but little change. 'Really it's them playing out in the studio, and I just have to capture that on to tape, so each project is the same in that respect. You're just capturing what they're giving you. [But] working with the trio of the Young brothers – first off, Malcolm and Angus are joined at the hip, and to have the third brother now coming in presented a little different dynamic from past records I'd worked on.'

That said, ultimately he also 'found it to be a bit easier because there was a lot of stuff went unsaid and was just understood between the three of them, because they'd made so many records together in the past'.

Indeed, big brother George's intuitive understanding of

the essentials of AC/DC's brand of hard rock helped the band not only in achieving the minimalist sonics they were after, but also in achieving them at speed. As Angus explained, 'We don't like to spend more than six weeks on an album. We don't want to lose the freshness. Our musical ambition had always been to put down a whole album like it was done by Little Richard and them back in the '50s.'

An important element of the band's ability to move at such a quick pace in the studio came with their already having written most of the tracks. Malcolm told *Mojo* that, leading up to the new album, the band spent 'two of those years [on] tour ... [where] you're not allowed to put your feet up. We're always trying to write good songs – we've got this style of music that it's hard to come up with things that are different within it – and we can afford to take this extra time. But we're not idle. Three months after the end of the tour, me and Angus get together and jam again and try to write.'

Elaborating further to rock journalist Susan Masino, Angus singled out an important element of the brothers' writing process. 'We strive for consistency. We spend a lot of time working on it, but [you have to] come up with something that's a little bit different from what you've done before. You don't want to be a clone of what you were before.'

The band tracked at Bryan Adams's Warehouse Studios in Vancouver, Canada. According to its official website, its precise location is in one of the most interesting areas of the city, Gastown, among shops, restaurants and nightclubs. 'Built by the Oppenheimer family during the gold rush in the 1800s, its original purpose was a Klondike supply warehouse and it even served as Vancouver's first City Hall. It is now the oldest brick building in Vancouver with restorations to both inside and out that have retained the historical integrity of the original structure.'

'The inside is a blend of modern amenities and state-of-the-art recording equipment. The Warehouse Studios started in the late 1987 in a basement of a house owned by multi-platinum Canadian rocker Bryan Adams, and ten years later, on 9 July 1997, we opened the doors at this Powell Street location. Studio 2 was completed on 9 February 1998 and Studio 1 was up and running on 18 October 1999. Technical and acoustic layout by Ron O Vermeulen. We have three studios, located on separate floors, which are comfortable and spacious with lots of natural light, each has a private kitchen and lounge area.'

Legendary record producer Bob Clearmountain (Bruce Springsteen, the Rolling Stones, Kiss, David Bowie, Bon Jovi and many more), who has worked out of the studio for more than 20 years, described the layout to *Mix* magazine. 'Touring the place, one is impressed by the lack of small rooms and tight hallways we studio moles have grown accustomed to. The lounges are large and bright, as are the control rooms and the one main recording room. No claustrophobia possible here. The stairways are open steel structures that add to the "warehouse" feel, but in a very *Architectural Digest* sort of way.'

In the same article, Adams himself said of his vision for the studio that 'it was passion – which in itself is a sort of mental illness – that drove me out of my home studio into this venture ... It seemed like the right way to go.' Studio 2 houses an SSL 9080J console and, he said, the company 'had been very good to me, and I always had trusted their products. I had no reason to believe their latest desk would be anything less than brilliant. It sounds amazing. I've done three albums on it, and all of them sound great. There are two recording rooms adjacent to the main studio. They ... have a similar ambience to the other studios.'

Studio A, where the band tracked between September and October 1999, has a Neve 8078 console and enormous speakers. 'They are,' Adams said, 'without a doubt the best large speakers I have ever heard in a control room. They crank!'

The Neve console, the proud owner went on, originally came from Air Studios in London. 'There were three desks built for Air, two of which they sold for some weird reason. One still exists at Air, and the other went to Montserrat and then later to A&M, and this is the third one and the largest, with 58 inputs. They were designed by Rupert Neve, [engineer] Geoff Emerick and [producer] George Martin to the best of my knowledge.'

'I first recorded on this exact desk in Atlantic Studios in New York when I was working with Joe Cocker on his album at the time. Later, I heard that Atlantic went under and the desk had been sold to a company called QSound. They had intended to put together a studio, but, at the last minute, they changed their minds. So, QSound gave me a day to decide if I wanted it. So I bought it and it sat in my warehouse for ages while Ron [Vermeulen] cleaned it up and waited for the studio to be built.'

'We've never regretted that purchase. Man, what a fantastic desk: it sounds unreal. Rupert Neve actually signed a plate for us, which is mounted on the right corner. We tried to make the desk as compatible with SSL engineers as possible. To do this, we put an SSL compressor in the desk, just like ordinary SSLs, and we also have several "Sneve" modules that Ron Vermeulen designed placed at the far end. A "Sneve" is an SSL module dressed up and fitted to look like a Neve module. It's useful if you are an engineer and you want to use the SSL sound for something.'

'As far as the room is concerned, it was delicate construction taking out the third floor of the building to allow us maximum ceiling height (25 feet). Other than that, we put in various angles on the isolation booths and retractable curtains and blinds, but left the room to be the room. It sounded fab.'

Of the rest of the studio's layout, Adams explained that

Warehouse had two mix rooms (Studios Two and Three) with an SSL J Series and SSL G+ respectively. 'In the main room, we have the analogue 11/44-inch with two Scully 11/44-inch machines locked up in sync … we have been with Apogee since the beginning with the AD/DA-500s … All of the rooms are interlocked to each other, including the Pro Tools room. It is sort of essential to do these days, especially when you have a group in using two rooms at a time, or to download a track to a Pro Tools operator and still continue to mix or record.'

'It was a great plan … isolation booths from Power Station, a Neve recording room like Air Studios in Oxford Street, a fantastic collection of vintage and modern equipment like A&M, and huge spaces to work in like the Sony film stage in LA. I think we have a great balance of all of the above.'

In detailing how the studio's layout worked to the band's advantage, Mike Fraser explained that, while Studio A at Warehouse is a fairly big room, 'more importantly has a special feature where we can build little rooms within a room, sort of gazebo-type structures where we can add a roof and a doorway. That's always what we do with AC/DC, because they like their drum sound really tight and in your face, so you have the drums right there in a small room, with the rest of the band set up in the rest of the big room. It's really important for them to have visual and close contact with the other guys, which is how they play so well – it's all done with eye contacts or a nod of the head or whatever, and that's how they do it live. They feel and sense each other being close by. You couldn't have Angus and Malcolm off in another room – it just wouldn't work for them because they always play together.'

'The album was tracked on a Neve console, and there's only three of this type in the world. They're quite special and they sound amazing, and, while it's still the same Neve EQ, this console has its own brand of EQ, with 4 ban EQ.'

Offering an insider's perspective on how AC/DC adapted the atmosphere of Adams's studio, Brian Johnson revealed to rock journalist Paul Stenning that 'it was kind of strange. I didn't know it was his until we were recording, and one day, in walks Bryan Adams. Apparently, he's a non-smoking vegetarian, and here [I am] … cooking all this meat and making bacon sandwiches. With this bacon smell floating around everywhere, he walks into the studio and it's full of cigarette smoke. So that was his introduction to us.'

Once attention had turned to tracking Angus and Malcolm's guitar interplay – the musical core of any AC/DC album – Angus told journalist Engleheart what he thought made the two siblings work so well together on album after album. 'I've been a little bit lucky for myself, probably from the beginning, because I've always had Malcolm. I could dream up some big idea some time and he'd tell me if it was stupid or something. Other times he'd go, "That's not bad," and he would make it happen. He's probably more practical than me. I'm a bit of a dreamer so I'm lucky in that sense.'

Further aiding that creative sound-boarding was brother George, who Angus credited with an ability to 'plug into me and Malcolm and keep us at bay sometimes too, when we want to kick the shit out of each other! So he's a bit of a mix of me and Malcolm – it's a funny thing.'

Engineer Mike Fraser certainly appreciated George's creative interventions as producer. 'Malcolm and Angus get along great as brothers, [but] sometimes there's disagreements, and having George there was great because he could referee a little. "OK you guys – off to your own corners and let's get this done." Not that it ever got literally to that point, but there was that dynamic there, and George being their older brother, there was a lot of respect there as well.'

Angus felt that George played an equally important role where rhythm was concerned. 'George knows his rhythm,' he told Engleheart. 'That's all you've got to have in this band, and a lot of producers don't have that. They've got the ears and timing, but no rhythm. It's mathematics to them; they don't understand the swing.'

Fraser offered a specific example of how this worked in action. 'Any time George had a suggestion, even if it was off the wall or something, they'd listen because George has been there right from the inception and has a lot of history with them. So they were a little bit quicker to listen to what he said, as opposed to another producer who might make a suggestion, and Angus and Malcolm might say, "Hmm, no – this is how we want to do it."

'There were times, for instance, where George might say, "Hey, guys – I think the tempo's wrong on that," and, even if they were hearing it a little bit differently, they would give his suggestions a try. And sometimes it would work out, for example with the title track "Stiff Upper Lip", which was originally played quite a lot faster than it ended up on the record, and George had an influence on that.'

Despite tracking live off the floor as always, drummer Phil Rudd faced one departure from his normal recording routine with the addition of a click track. 'We've never used a click on any song, on any album while I've been with the band,' he said to *Rhythm* magazine. 'When we got George Young back as producer, we both rose to the occasion and there was huge admiration right around the camp.'

What did stay business-as-usual on *Stiff Upper Lip*, Phil added to *Musician* magazine, was the overall rhythm of the band staying within 'the straight feel. The guys write these riffs and all I have to do is whomp it in the middle. That is what I like.'

Even with the advent of Pro Tools, which engineer Fraser used in recording the album, the band insisted on tracking takes from top to bottom. 'I remember one song when we were doing *Stiff Upper Lip*, the take was great, but the take after that they liked the last chorus and the whole outro better –

they thought it had better energy. So on the tape we physically spliced those two together, and nobody could tell the tempo changed, but there was a little change in it and it didn't flow as well. They said, "Nope, go with the other take then." They like to do it live – they don't like to manufacture it. There's nothing faked, and the only overdubs are Brian's vocals and Angus's leads or flourishes. The basic two rhythm guitars, bass and drums are always one live take with no editing. They never go back in and redo their performances again – it's all live off the floor, and that's the great thing about that band.'

When it came time to pick a title for the album, the band's consensus was squarely on *Stiff Upper Lip*. 'There was a bit of humour [in that],' Angus admitted to Engleheart. 'Even from when we started, I used to always say, "I've got bigger lips than Jagger and I've got bigger lips than Presley when I stick them out."'

As for the label's decision to push the title track as the album's first single, Brian Johnson told journalist Stenning, '"Stiff Upper Lip" was great, but I would have chosen "Can't Stand Still" because it didn't have a high and low – just simple, straightahead rock. It just rocks. I'm amazed that it wasn't taken out as a single. We did that all the way through without any breaks – it's just beautiful rock 'n' roll.'

Respect from the media was duly forthcoming. *Rolling Stone* noted that 'with older brother George Young back on board as producer, *Stiff Upper Lip* wisely [sticks] ... to its time-tested formula of no-frills riffing' and concluded that it 'confirmed AC/DC's status as one of the most enduringly popular hard-rock bands on the planet'. *Entertainment Weekly* celebrated the band's return to 'bluesy barroom rock ... [that] makes zero concessions to contemporary metal's low-tuned terror. It's refreshing that these anthems would be at home on 1980's *Back in Black*.' *New Musical Express* closed out the critical chorus of praise by urging its readers to buy the album NOW if they knew what was good for them, and declaring, 'Let's not piss about. You can debate this and argue that but certain things we hold to be self-evident and one of those things is that AC/DC are the fuckin' greatest.'

As for the band themselves, they seemed quite satisfied with the results they'd produced. Drummer Phil Rudd told *Rhythm* magazine, 'I love the album, I really do. I play it all the time if I'm at home or in the car. All the songs are really good.'

'We know what we do best, which is rock 'n' roll,' Angus told journalist Masino, adding in a poignant postscript, 'I think he [Bon Scott] would've been proud, just knowing how he was as a person. So I always think he would look well on what we've done and I believe he does now, in a way.'

Debuting at No. 7 on the Billboard Top 200 Album Chart in December 2002, *Stiff Upper Lip* would be certified platinum within six months of its release. Its success reflected what the Detroit *Metro Times* pointed to in its album review as a remarkable longevity that 'after 27 years...[leaves] little doubt that AC/DC stands as perhaps the greatest living breathing, hard-rock band'.

Part of why this stayed true album after album came with the fact that, as Brian Johnson explained to journalist Paul Stenning, 'AC/DC has survived because we've never changed direction, never given in to trends. That's why there haven't been any solo projects from within the band. No one has ever wanted to. Our music doesn't go out of fashion because it isn't about fashion. I hear about all these different kinds of music – grunge, hardcore, death metal. And all it is is rock 'n' roll … Our music comes from the heart. It's always been there. People put you down for playing rock 'n' roll, you know? Well, fuck those people. You have got to do your own thing.'

Following the release of *Stiff Upper Lip*, AC/DC left their longtime American label Elektra. In December 2002, they signed what *Billboard* magazine called 'a multi-album deal with Epic, the first fruit of which will be refurbished reissues of seminal albums such as *Back in Black*, *Highway to Hell* and *Dirty Deeds Done Dirt Cheap* … Further reissues will follow, all of which will sport new liner notes and rare photos, and utilise Sony's proprietary ConnecteD technology to unlock special online content created for each release.'

'The group's back catalogue is one of the most consistent sellers on Billboard's Top Pop Catalogue chart. According to Epic parent Sony, 1980's *Back in Black* has sold 41 million copies worldwide, making it the sixth highest-selling album in history. It has sold 318,000 copies this year alone, according to Nielsen SoundScan.

'The move to Epic reunites AC/DC with Epic chairman Dave Glew, who previously worked with the group at Atlantic, as well as Epic executive VP/GM Steve Barnett, formerly the group's manager. The new deal brings 16 of AC/DC's 18 US releases to the label, which plans to also reissue some of the albums on vinyl and compile DVD releases.'

The band's home newspaper, Australia's *Daily Telegraph*, added of the deal's details that 'the band is expected to generate sales worth up to $100 million annually for their new label Sony Music. AC/DC will continue to be released by their original Australian label Albert Productions here, which is currently distributed by the Festival Mushroom Group.'

Though the deal was a lucrative one, it would be more than six years before Epic got their first album, as the band took some time off to pursue their individual passions. For Brian Johnson, in addition to his Formula 1 racing team, these artistic extracurricular activities included composing the music for a new musical project inspired by the Ancient Greek legend of Helen of Troy. As reported by Playbill.com, 'Johnson's collaborators on the project include fellow musician Brendan Healy, and the book-writing team of Dick Clement and Ian La Frenais, screenwriters of the film *The Commitments*. The score is described as a mix of rock 'n' roll,

R&B and pop. As the title amply suggests, the show takes its inspiration from the classical tale of Helen, for whom a thousand Greek ships sailed to war against Troy.'

'His background notwithstanding, Johnson said in a statement, "I love musical theatre, especially the classic stuff, like Rodgers and Hammerstein."'

Going into greater depth about his inspiration for the idea, Brian told the *Sunday Times* that 'one day I was sitting through [Andrew Lloyd Webber's musical *Cats*] and thought, "I can do better than this." I thumbed through the programme and there was an advertisement for a bank with gold coins tumbling out of a wooden horse. That triggered the idea for Helen of Troy. It was as simple as that.'

At the time of writing, the musical has yet to be produced commercially, although songs from it were previewed in New York in 2005. Some of the music also appeared in one episode of the TV series *Goddess Odyssey,* in which Brian made a light-hearted visit to Greece in search of shrines, temples and paths relating to the legend of Helen of Troy. The episode was released on DVD in 2005 as *Goddess Odyssey — Path of Helen of Troy*.

CHAPTER FOURTEEN

BLACK ICE (2008)

'The critics have always been a little flippant with
AC/DC about Angus ... It's always easy to have
a quick little joke or dig at the expense of it,
the easy riffs, the such and such, and they're all dead
wrong. The easiest riffs in the world are the hardest
ones to write, because they are very few'
BRIAN JOHNSON

Black ice, by general definition, describes slippery road
conditions – hard to detect and potentially lethal. That's
exactly what almost any band would face commercially
after almost a decade off between new studio albums – but
not AC/DC.

When the band entered the studio in 2007 to begin tracking
their 17th studio album in 35 years, longtime engineer Mike
Fraser remembered feeling that, although 'nine years had
passed between albums, it was like no time had lapsed at all'.
The band had the same desire to capture their signature sound
on *Black Ice* – 'just rock 'n' roll' as Angus told journalist Ethan
Schlesinger. 'A lot of times we get criticised for it. A lot of
music papers come out with "When are they going to stop
playing these three chords?" If you believe you shouldn't play

just three chords, it's pretty silly on their part. To us, the simpler a song is, the better, 'cause it's more in line with what the person on the street is.'

Angus revealed to rock writer Murray Engleheart that, in writing for the band's first studio album in almost a decade, the mainstay process was still rooted in the creative kinship he had with his brother Malcolm. 'If we come up with ideas and stuff, I'll look at Malcolm and every time it amazes me. I'll sit and hear what he's got – an idea off a tape or something – and it's always different. It's way ahead and in front of anyone I've ever met. It's unique.

'I like tapping my foot. For me, if you give me just a straight-out rock 'n' roll tune I'm happy, whether it's a "T.N.T." or a "Whole Lotta Rosie" or something like this, or a "Highway to Hell" where it's just straight[forward] – that's what I love best. But Malcolm always looks – he'll try and be one step ahead with the approach and he'll tell you, "Look, Ang – you've done that before" or "We've done that."'

Brian Johnson – in an interview with Triple M Radio Australia – gave credit to the brothers for always having new ideas. 'They always have something new. That's why there's never been a Greatest Hits. We've been asked plenty of times but they just shake their heads and go, "No, I've got some new riffs – let's get into the studio."'

Though the brothers strove to keep their ideas fresh, Angus did share with the *Sun* that, in the course of pre-production writing for *Black Ice*, the band's new material also 'had to be representative of how we are. We had other songs but they weren't right. Every one of the 15 tracks on *Black Ice*, you will say, "That is AC/DC."'

Whereas with past albums the band had been rushing to keep songs coming during gruelling tours, Angus told music writer Paul Cashmere that this time around they felt they'd earned the right to take their time. 'AC/DC have made more albums in our career than a lot of bands have done. We have had more albums in the last 20 years than The Who. We are now lucky we get a lot more time to sit back and spend the time writing, which is great for us. You can really concentrate. Sometimes in the past you got the deadline coming into it, especially when you commit yourself to a tour. A lot of stuff in the early days was written and recorded while we were touring. Nowadays, it's good to be able to sit back and pick what we want to do.'

Engineer Mike Fraser added, 'I think they just love doing music and being out there, even though it's a two-and-a-half- to three-year grind for them living on the road. They just love playing so much that I think they came back to do this record for that reason.'

Once the band had arrived in London to begin work on the album, Fraser recalled that 'they hadn't done any rehearsing or pre-production at all – they all flew in from different parts of the world and said, "Hey, let's do a record."'

'Angus and Malcolm write, and bounce ideas off each other. They have a little studio in England, so they go in and record quick writing demos, and bring those ideas on their computers. So just before we'd do a take, they'd play it to the rest of the band, explain "Here's the riff, here's the chord progression, etc." I remember before we started tracking the first song, I was sitting there thinking to myself, "This should be interesting. Nine years they haven't played together – maybe it will be a little rough at first." But right from the first get-go, it was on. It was like "Holy shit! These guys are so good, they can take nine years off, barely warm up and away they go." They were just amazing that way!'

Before entering the studio, Fraser and his co-producer – Atlanta-born Brendan O'Brien (Pearl Jam, Rage Against the Machine, Stone Temple Pilots, Korn) – had their own soundman version of pre-production to divvy up the recording responsibilities. 'It must have been a funny thing to walk into,' Fraser said. 'I've worked with the band for so many years, and he's walking in brand new – first time he's met the band. And they've got me there, and Brendan's an engineer himself, so for the band to insist on having me there was probably a bit overcoming for him to walk in on. But again, he's a professional and we all got along great.'

'I remember when he first came in, we talked about the approach of the record and whatnot. He said, "I know you've worked with them in the past, so I'm just gonna let you do your thing. But I'm an engineer too, so just so you know there might be times I'm gonna jump on the board and change a few things. Are you cool with that?" And I said, "Of course. We're here to do a record together – there's no ego."

'It actually ended up that he didn't do that too much. We quickly earned each other's respect, and had a great time working together. There's a little bit of "feeling out" time, and Brendan was a big AC/DC fan as well, so the first couple days of working with them I imagine was probably a little bit intimidating. But he's a great producer, and was really good at pulling the best out of those guys in the studio. My being as intimately familiar with the band as an engineer helped to free Brendan up to focus more on production. An engineer's role is to be a liaison between the band and producer, and on *Black Ice* that was even more the case, because I'd worked so much with the band and understood their sound. I think, in that respect, Brendan quite enjoyed being able to just be the producer, and not have to worry about other things. He knew I had his back.'

Brian Johnson described the band's introduction to their new producer to the *Sun*: 'There was a little awkwardness when you first get in the studio with a new guy because he's butting into your little gang. But, by Christ, after five minutes with this guy we could see how wonderful he was. Brendan was fantastic.'

Angus added to rock journalist Susan Masino that 'it was a good experience … working with Mike Fraser again. It was also very good to work with Brendan O'Brien, who has a musician's background. Communicating with someone like that is also very good, because he knows exactly what you need. He knows what you're talking about. He is very, very sharp.'

AC/DC soon got down to work, mapping out their goals for the album. 'Consciously,' Fraser said, 'I think we all talked about the fact that *Stiff Upper Lip* was a record that they wanted to make a little drier and more bluesier, which was a departure from their usual direction, but, on *Black Ice*, they wanted to get back on track with their classic sound. With the songs in such a new stage, Brendan would help a little bit with some of the arrangements, and suggest, "Well, let's do that six times here instead of the four times." He had quite a soft touch with them, because AC/DC doesn't really need to be produced. They just want sort of a collaborative effort to get the best down on tape, and Brendan handled that great.'

Angus told journalist Paul Cashmere that he'd been 'impressed by [O'Brien] because he is a musician first and has great production skills. We told him to be brutal.'

'His being a guitar player really helped meld him in with the band and earn their respect,' Fraser agreed. 'He would listen to one of their writing demos on the laptop, then he and the band would sit together and he'd say, "Yeah, that's really good, but I would get to the chorus faster," or "Let's do a double-chorus here." The band would quickly try his idea out on acoustic guitars and, if they liked it, they'd go with it. He'd also help them work out a tempo, or say, "We need a mid-tempo song, so let's try this one out," and that kind of thing – just helping to guide the process as opposed to trying to take it over.'

For O'Brien, his desire to work with AC/DC began with personal sentiment as a fan: 'I missed AC/DC, and wanted the same band back.'

Brian Johnson felt this correlated directly with the band's own desires, telling LA radio station KLSX Free FM that 'he knows exactly what we want'.

In an interview with the *Atlanta Constitution* newspaper, O'Brien recalled that 'going into it, there were no real expectations because I literally met them the first day of recording. Their people called my people and they wanted me to work with them on the new record. They hadn't made a record in seven or eight years and the last few records they'd done, though they were good records, they hadn't been received as well as other ones had been. I didn't know what to expect, but the first day we got together, Angus and Malcolm sat down and played me a bunch of demos and I was pretty encouraged by them. As soon as they started playing, it was obvious they still sounded great, they still had it and it was just a matter of trying to return them to form a bit.'

The band entered Warehouse Studios in Vancouver in March 2008 to begin principal tracking. Now recording to Pro Tools, Fraser explained, 'I separated my drum tracks a little more than

BLACK ICE (2008)

I would have done back in the 24-track tape days, because you're more limited. I always keep the kick separate, and I like the two snare mics separate. A lot of times, say if there's three or four tom mics, I will bounce down to a stereo pair, just to save a few tracks. With all the overheads and close stuff, I'll usually put them down to a stereo pair, then usually throw up a couple of room mics. I use basically the same mics on AC/DC's drums as I always have.'

'With each record you mix a little bit differently. With that band, they do have their sound and haven't really changed that fundamentally, but, if you listen to their catalogue of records in chronological order, the sound does change a bit in the mix. But again, one of the very cool things about AC/DC, and part of why they have so many fans, is that they don't stray away from what they are – they don't go with the trends. So the changes in their sound come more with the fact that they might be recording in different rooms from album to album, but their fundamental sound is the same.'

Another mainstay – tracking the band on the Neve console in Studio One – was fine with Fraser. 'I love the sound of the Neve desk,' he told *Sound on Sound* magazine, 'and from there everything went straight to the studio's Studer A800 Mk3 24-track. Neve gear going into an analogue tape machine, and then mixing on an SSL, as I did for this album – for me, that's the sound of rock 'n' roll.'

'Analogue tape just has a sound to it. Analogue records

frequencies outside the human hearing range that filter down and are audible as sub-harmonics, and this makes a big difference for the sound. Even though digital is getting closer with HD, it still sounds quite grainy to me and the top end has little teeth on it, whereas the high end of analogue is smooth and silky. I think the sub-harmonics fill in those little sawtooth grooves. Also, tape has its own compression. There are plug-ins that simulate this, but it's still not the same thing.'

'Of course, there are problems with tape as well. You have more hiss, so the noise floor is louder, and it's not so easy to edit. You also don't have as many tracks. With AC/DC we ended up with maybe 12 to 14 backing tracks per song, and I transferred these over to Pro Tools for the vocal and guitar overdubs. The main reason was that you don't want to get cramped when you do multiple overdub takes. We decided not to go too crazy – we wanted it easy as well. And Pro Tools was easier for editing. There may have been a song where we took a chorus from one take and edited that with another take, but we didn't chop anything up and comp things. Overall, I used Pro Tools purely as a tape machine, also during the mix.'

Commenting on the band's desire to stick with the sound that had worked for them over the better part of four decades, drummer Phil Rudd told *Rhythm* magazine that 'so many groups try different directions and they don't really work. We just stick to our guns!'

This philosophy would win fans and critics over, with the *Village Voice* noting of *Black Ice* that its 'groove comes courtesy of Ang's brother/guitarist Malcolm and the rhythm section of bassist Cliff Williams and drummer Phil Rudd, the latter of whom is a marvel of simplicity. The man's got basically one pattern in his arsenal, but it's a knockout: kick on the 1 and 3, snare on the 2 and 4, hi-hat all the way through to provide a bit of shimmy. He manages to both swing and plod simultaneously, while staying forever rock steady.'

Fraser felt that 'there's such an honest approach: "This is what we are, this is what we like, and this is what how we like to do it." Over the years, they haven't really changed their style much. And some people will say, "Yeah, but they only play three chords," but that is their formula of rock. That sound has crossed over a lot of age groups and genres, and because they aren't trying to be trendy at all, they just play honestly what they want – it's just good old, foot-stompin' fun music.'

When attention turned to laying down Angus and Malcolm's guitar tracks, the latter recalled that upon entering the studio – even after such a long break from recording – the band stuck 'to the same sounds... We put our amps on the same setting every night and ... we put out the same album every year with a different cover. We're not about sitting around climbing up our own arse. Basically we're a two-guitar band with three or four chords, though we might add another one if we're feeling tricky.'

The *Sunday Times* might hail Angus's solos as a 'guitar firestorm' and *Entertainment Weekly* declare they erupt 'like the baby monster pummelling its way through John Hurt's chest in *Alien*', but the lead guitarist, as always, defined his role as part of the band. 'We all play together,' he told *Guitar Player*. 'The guys all around me – it's just like a team... [so] that's hard because I never look at them as a solo thing.'

Elaborating, Angus added that, as with all the band's past albums, 'I'm just like a colour over the top. [Malcolm's] the solid thing; he pumps it along. His right hand is always going. In that field I don't think anyone can do what he does. He's very clean; he's very hard. It's an attack. Anyone that sees him or knows about guitars can tell.'

Mike Fraser shared this opinion. 'Malcolm is one of the best rhythm guitar players I think I've ever worked with. His sense of rhythm and groove is amazing, and, if you watch AC/DC live, most of the guys in the band will watch Malcolm for all the cues and tempos and all that stuff.'

'It's quite funny, because, when he's solo, Malcolm's is a very, very clean sound, and other bands come in the studio and say, "Oh, we want this AC/DC sound" and they've got this really overdriven thing, which is not the case at all in reality. Malcolm has a really clean, almost shiny sound, and Angus has a crunchy sound that isn't overly distorted. Somehow when those two are meshed together, it creates the illusion that it's bigger than it really is. I think that's the secret of their sound – less is more. We just end up getting such a bigger sound when we don't have to layer all these guitar parts.'

In tracking the brothers, Fraser took a similarly defined technical approach. 'With all the records I've done, Malcolm's on the left side, and Angus is always on the right. There's always only the two guitar parts. Sometimes if the song needs it, Angus will play a single power chord track, and that will be panned right in the middle, but way back in the mix so it doesn't clutter. The only other overdubs are Angus's little leads or flourishes, but it's basically Malcolm on one side, Angus on the other, no double tracking or anything. Angus and Malcolm's interplay together as guitar players is really uncanny and that's why they're such a great band. Because they're brothers it's so instinctive.'

From a technical perspective, the engineer added that with 'each guitar part I like to keep to one track, but sometimes I'll do a separate track with a room sound I'm not sure I want to use quite yet. But when I record tracks, I like to get them down on tape the way I want the balances to be. I don't want to record all these mics on separate tracks, then have somebody else come along and redo the balance if they're going to be mixing it later. I want to lock in an idea that "This is what we're going for, this is what we want." At the same time, keeping my options open too, so I wouldn't record a big giant room sound on the guitar track, and then later on go, "Oh, I want it to be dry now." Well, you can't undo that. So I would put a room track on a separate channel to protect that option.'

In an interview with *Sound on Sound* magazine, Fraser offered additional details about recording the band's guitars. 'Obviously we had the guitar and bass cabinets in the iso[lation] booths to reduce spill … In addition, one thing that I have learned from working with AC/DC over the years is to try and keep the cables from the guitar to the amp head and from the amp to the cabinet as short as possible. So they had their amp heads with them in the live room. With short cables, you get all the bottom end as well as a nice top end. As soon as you lengthen the cable, the magic of the sound goes away and you have to add more top end at the amp, or EQ on the desk, and the sound becomes fuzzy as opposed to crunchy. A lot of people ask me how I get such a huge guitar sound, and it's simply Malcolm in one speaker and Angus in the other, and there are no effects. The short cables are one of the main reasons.'

The engineer also emphasised the band's preference for staying connected throughout the album's recording. 'All five members of the band had headphones. The Warehouse has a headphone system in which every musician has his own little mini-mixer. I sent them four tracks of drums – kick, snare, and stereo drums – plus guitar, guitar, bass, vocal and talkback mic. Brendan would sit in the room with them and also had headphones on, and he had a little talkback mic and would coach them on the new stuff, reminding them things like "OK, here comes the verse."

'This recording setup remained the same for the whole album. We recorded in batches of three songs, laying down the backing tracks for them, then we'd take a break, and then Brian would add his vocals, Angus would do his lead overdubs, and we'd do background vocals. Once the songs were pretty complete, though not yet finished, we'd do another batch of three songs. This was to keep things interesting. Otherwise, Brian would have had to do two weeks of vocals overdubs and Angus would have been playing solos for two weeks.'

When the production team moved from the main room into the control room for Angus's solos, the engineer recalled that, as always, when Angus was plugged in and tape was rolling, 'Malcolm is there holding down the groove and the rhythm, and that leaves the room for Angus to kind of put all the flourishes and whatnot in, and their two sounds really mash together nicely.'

For his soloing, Angus told *Gibson*, 'I just came up with something that fitted the mood of the song. A lot of the time I'd be thinking of something very complex but, usually, the best thing was the thing that was simple, because it cut right through. So I always thought that was the best approach.' He added that, as spontaneity was king during recording, 'I never worked [out solo parts] unless there's an important part, like if it's part of the song.'

Brian Johnson's Herculean vocal efforts received the appropriate chorus of accolade from impressed critics. *Billboard* observed in their review that 'front man Brian Johnson is in fine form', while the *Washington Post* noted that Johnson 'sings more and hollers less' and that his vocals had helped to 'carry *Black Ice* on their back'.

In an interview with Triple M Radio Australia, Johnson admitted having had initial concerns about whether he'd be able to rise to the occasion. 'When we were about to start this album I really did wonder if I could do it. It's not only doing the new songs, it's having to sing songs the way you sang them 30 years ago … If the body or the voice packs in, there's nothing I can do. I'll go on as long as I can … Thankfully the old tubes have held up. They've got a little bluesier – that just happens with life. I'm just happy I can still do it, but believe you me, I'll jump ship the first time I let anybody down.'

That commitment to delivering the best performance possible led Brian to recall to *Reader's Digest* a specific request to producer Brendan O'Brien before he started the album. 'I said, "Brendan, will you make me a promise? If I'm not up to scratch, if I'm not up to the job, please tell me! I'm a big boy, I won't cry, I'll just disappear. I'll just say goodbye to the boys, and they can get somebody else in to do the job." And I really, really mean it. Because the last thing I want is to be the member in this band that holds it all back. So Brendan looked at me and he went, "OK." But he never said anything, so I was very lucky.'

Crediting Johnson with far more than luck in keeping his vocal cords healthy in the years in between albums, Fraser recalled that 'when we were doing *Black Ice*, there had been about nine years in between records. When he isn't singing, Brian owns a racing team, and races almost at the Formula 1 level, and the guy has six-pack abs, and is in just great shape for a 63-year-old guy. So when he was tracking vocals this time around, being in such good shape, he actually had more power and more stamina in his singing than he's ever had.'

Indeed, Johnson confirmed in an interview with the *Sun*, 'I've been working out and I'm getting the fitness guru for Formula 1 to come in and knock the stuffing out of us for a couple of weeks. I'm scared. He's a toughie. But you know, I work out three days a week and I run six days a week to try to keep me fitness levels up.'

Even so, the production team were constantly conscious of what Fraser identified as overworking him. 'With his style as a vocalist, for really any age, you just have to be really careful not to over-sing him, so I only record him for maybe an hour to hour and a half a day, not wanting to burn his throat out. When he's getting tired in his throat, you have to rest him, because, when he sings, there's so much power coming out of him. If you push him, it will take him two or three days to recover from that. That's really the only thing I have to watch with him.'

Recalling some of the vocal-tracking tricks that Brendan O'Brien brought to the console, Johnson told the *Sun*, 'He would never call you by your first name but by both names. He goes, "Brian Johnson – are you ready to sing?" Well, yeah, sure I am, Brendan. "OK, let's go down there – see what you got, big boy." Then looking at me, he said, "Brian Johnson, you don't like singing in studios, do ya?" and I said, "No, I frickin' hate it." He said, "What's wrong?" I said, "It's the buttons, it's the microphone hanging down, it's the headphones and then it's the 1, 2, 3 and sing." So, he said, "Just give me a night to think about it."

'The next day I came in and he said, "OK, this is the room you're gonna sing in." I went, "But this is the office behind the reception desk in the studio." He said, "Yeah, well, you said you didn't like to be alone." So he put a couple of speakers and a little mixing desk in there and gave me this huge microphone, this big old Shure 56 which weighed about seven pounds, and he said, "OK, let's rock." He played the backing track the boys had done the night before and I started singing … and the receptionist resigned immediately. The poor little girl, she got the shock of her life and she had a German Shepherd dog which started howling. I don't know if he was joining in or he was protesting about the whole thing!'

The *Guardian* would later hail his vocals as 'stoked up on rock 'n' roll steam' and Johnson himself felt impressed by the results. 'When I heard the album, I was stunned,' he told the *Sun*. 'It was almost like listening to myself 30 years ago. It honestly feels like a young band who have just come on the scene.'

When principal tracking had wrapped, attentions turned to mixing. The Warehouse's mixing room, as owner Bryan Adams proudly pointed out, now has the AD8000 for 5.1 mixing and the latest PSX-100s in all rooms, for 24-bit, 96k mixing. It also features large windows to allow in maximum light. In Adams's opinion, 'Daylight and a view on to the street are perfect in the recording studio, especially with the urban vibe where we are. It's colourful out there. Plus, I learned from my home studio [which] had a fantastic view over the garden and the bay. I wanted to peer out at something when I was working... We have portable large monitors that go in there if someone needs them.'

At the end of the day, according to Fraser, when mixing AC/DC the bottom line is emphasising the instruments that are driving the song. 'Drums obviously, but sometimes the guitar parts are a little more riffy, so the bass can be back in the mix, or sometimes, as was the case with "Anything Goes", the bass line really helps carry that song. So because it needed the bass out there to help drive the song, that's the direction we went in. But generally, in mixes, the band likes the bass sort of as a background role.'

In a separate interview with *Sound on Sound*, Fraser added that, when he started mixing, Brendan and Brian were still overdubbing vocals in the editing suite downstairs while he was mixing upstairs in Studio Three. 'They would come up towards the end of the day to check my mix, and we would move on to the next song the following day. I don't really like to have people around when I mix. Not that I have any tricks or secrets, but I need people to walk in with fresh ears. You're sitting there a whole day working hard on it, and by the end of the day you may be adding too much top end because your ears are getting tired, or maybe your perspective is shifting a little bit. Also, they don't want to sit around a whole day listening to me soloing a kick or a snare drum!

'In addition, I find that, when I mix something that I've also recorded, I sometimes overdo it. I'm used to working hard on mixes that I didn't record, but with my own stuff I have to remember just to mix it, and not EQ it like crazy to make something happen. After having worked on a project for six weeks or so, it may not sound as exciting as when you first heard it, but that's just in your head. So it's always good to have fresh ears coming in.'

Using the album's biggest hit single as an example of his approach to mixing on *Black Ice*, Fraser explained, 'On the multitrack tape for "Rock 'n' Roll Train" we had two tracks each of overheads, kick, snare, toms and room, and one track of hi-hat and ride, totalling 12 tracks, plus two tracks of guitars and two of bass, so 16 tracks in total. In Pro Tools I also had two tracks of lead vocals, two tracks of lead guitar, and two or three tracks of backing vocals. One of the challenges in mixing AC/DC is to make sure everything is right on your face with only a few instruments. With most bands you have lots of tracks, which initially is harder to mix, but once everything is up and balanced, then that's your mix.'

'The rhythm guitars are absolutely bone dry. On the intros of some of the songs I added some EMT 140 plate reverb on the guitar if it was Angus by himself. His solo guitar would have had a Studer tape slap delay on it, about 140ms, the same as I used on Brian's vocal. Reverbs are usually too washy for my taste, but sometimes bone dry doesn't give you the emotion you want. In that case a delay can work. There are no effects on the bass guitar.'

'With AC/DC it can be a challenge to make sure the drums are thumping enough, and that the guitars and bass are also in your face enough. The guitars have such a large sound that, when you push them up, you lose the drums, so you push the drums up, but then you lose the bass, and so you push the bass up, and you keep pushing everything louder and louder, and suddenly you hit a wall and you have to start all over. That's the main challenge.'

'But I've mixed several records, I'm a fan, and I know how they should sound, so it was not too difficult... [In general] with AC/DC I simply put one rhythm guitar in each speaker. Often when I mix other people's stuff, the guitars will be in stereo, and then they'll have double-tracked them. In such a case it becomes a depth and a layer issue, which in the track doesn't actually sound that big. The thing about AC/DC is that they don't double-track their guitars. I keep saying to young bands: if you want a really big guitar sound, just get a really good mono guitar sound! Of course, when you double something, it sounds bigger, but in the end result you have less guitar: you have to turn it down because it takes up too much space in the stereo image. The other way to get a big guitar sound is to pan it.'

'Your kick and your snare and your bass will be in the middle, and your background vocals will be a little to the left and the right, and if you pan your guitars further out you get this whole wide spectrum of everything that's happening. In such a situation it's really easy to mix so that everything can be heard and everything sounds loud, instead of everything being on top of each other with lots of layers. I try to keep things clear and natural and open and as little processed as possible, because I think it just ends up sounding better. If I can get a good balance like this and it sounds great, I'm not going to bother with throwing all sorts of effects on the mix. I'm quite a minimalist when it comes to outboard gear. My assistant loves working with me, because when he's doing the recall notes for the mixes he always laughs and says, "There's nothing to write down!"'

'I mixed the whole album to half-inch at 30ips, and it was mastered from there. The band have released the album both on CD and on vinyl, and when I A/B'ed the CD against the vinyl, the latter sounded amazing. That's the difference between recording in analogue and in Pro Tools! I also didn't use plug-ins because I don't like working in the box, and they don't sound anywhere near the real thing.'

Ultimately, the team succeeded in creating an album that the *Village Voice* noted 'not only restores the pristine vintage Marshall guitar sound – bright, warm, ever so slightly overdriven – of the band's classic '70s efforts with producers Harry Vanda and big brother George Young, but also lifts a key element of their mega-selling Mutt Lange-produced trilogy: gigantic, gang-vocal-soaked choruses. O'Brien, to his credit, takes things even further here than Lange ever dared, pulling some unexpectedly musical aah-aah-aaahs out of the boys on "Smash 'n' Grab" and getting them chanting like a squad of high-school cheerleaders on "She Likes Rock 'n' Roll". Quality stuff.'

Brendan O'Brien offered his reflections on the album's warm reception to the *Atlanta Constitution*. 'I can't say it's completely unexpected because my feeling was that once an artist has established a sound, if you put out a record of songs that people like, whether you call them hits or whatever, people will respond. But I must tell you I did not expect it to be as overwhelming as it's been. I guess you could call it a full-blown phenomenon at this point because it's really blown up all over the world. And I can tell you that they are very gratified by the response and they're really excited about it, too.'

On its release on 20 October 2008, *Black Ice* made a No. 1 debut in the Billboard Top 200 Album Chart, with a remarkable 1,762,000 units sold worldwide, of which 784,000 were in the US alone. In its second week, the *LA Times* would report that 'AC/DC topped the one-million sales mark for its new *Black Ice* during the album's second week of release, holding on to the No. 1 spot on the national sales chart with 271,000 copies.'

While the success was gratifying for the band, Angus remained unfazed, telling *Undercover Australia*, 'We been there, seen there, done it. As far as for us, there is always a new band out there, this year's new thing. AC/DC is AC/DC and what the other guy does has never really bothered us. We have never had to have been in a competition.'

In fact, the main competition surrounding *Black Ice* was among the chorus of music critics singing the band's praises. *Billboard* hailed *Black Ice* as 'a 15-track extravaganza that frequently echoes the down-and-dirty rock 'n' roll of its iconic 1980 [predecessor] *Back in Black*'. The *Guardian* said that, 'much to their credit, AC/DC have stuck to their guns with electrifying results', while the BBC noted that 'sixteen albums in, AC/DC have no reason to tinker with a formula that was well-nigh perfect to begin with'.

In America, *Entertainment Weekly* added, 'The appeal of

BLACK ICE (2008)

AC/DC lies with their more-than-30-year-old commitment to the same no-frills metal groove.' The *New York Daily News* got its biggest kick out of the fact that while 'everyone fears change … imagine the power of being able to offer something that never does. That's the profound promise of AC/DC … [*Black Ice*] has the same gleaming features and signature force … it's thrilling in the extreme.'

The *Washington Post* would declare *Black Ice* to be 'the best record the band had made in decades', and the Grammy Awards would come to agree, honouring the band with their first ever award, appropriately for 'Best Hard Rock Performance' in 2009.

CONCLUSION

IRON MAN 2 (2010)

**'AC/DC may also be the purest way for anyone
to become interested in rock 'n' roll music'**
ANTIMUSIC.COM

By now, everyone on the rock 'n' roll globe has heard of, and probably banged their head or pumped their fist to, AC/DC. For the better part of four decades, they have turned out a signature brand of hard rock that lead singer Brian Johnson proudly declared to *Mojo* 'no one else can do … as good as this band!' The Rock 'n' Roll Hall of Fame, who inducted AC/DC in 2003, concluded the band was worthy of the honour because of an 'unwavering devotion to no-frills rock … that's won them the loyalty of millions of fans'.

It's a party any time AC/DC comes on the radio, iPod, jukebox or even the silver screen. In 2010, *Iron Man 2* featured a platinum-selling soundtrack stocked entirely with examples of AC/DC's brand of timeless rock 'n' roll dynamism. In April 2010, it made a No. 4 debut in the US Billboard Top 200 Album Chart, and reached No. 1 on the UK and Australian

Billboard Album Charts. The appetite for the band was equally voracious around the world: Mexico (No. 7), Hungary (No. 2), Ireland (No. 1), Canada (No. 2), Norway (No. 4), France (No. 5), Netherlands (No. 5), Finland (No. 14), Belgium (No. 22) and Poland (No. 34).

According to the *LA Times*, the band's enduring appeal has translated into AC/DC having 'outsold Madonna, Michael Jackson, the Rolling Stones, the Who and Led Zeppelin and is second in sales only to the Beatles', while the *Wall Street Journal* said the sales reflected 'the most popular back catalogue of any band other than the Beatles'. In addition to a juke-box full of hits, *Maxim* added that 'a series of killer albums and some of the loudest, most thrilling gigs in rock history [over] the past 25 years have seen the band cement their reputation as the greatest rock 'n' roll band the world has ever seen'. It's a fair bet that a hundred years from now, as different as the world might look, not much will have changed where fan love for AC/DC is concerned.

And still the band remains as musically and personally unassuming as their millions of fans around the world. Engineer Mike Fraser, who has spent a fair part of the past 20 years working alongside the band in the studio, hails the band as 'one of the most sweetheart bands I've ever worked alongside. They're just so down to earth, and there's no egos or anything like that about them. They're just absolutely lovely people to work with.'

Keeping both feet firmly planted in the rock 'n' roll soil they have been cultivating for years, AC/DC no doubt still have more anthems to support what MTV argues is a 'strong case for claiming the title of greatest rock band around'.

Indeed, Angus would 'like to be around a few years, still banging away but not being boring. I just want to go further – make more noise.'

The band's rock 'n' roll longevity, Brian Johnson reasoned to MMM Radio Australia, is because 'we're very hard to get rid of. AC/DC are a bit like them bugs, the cockroaches. Nothing can kill us.' The singer concluded by posing the simplest but perhaps most poignant question of all about AC/DC's ultimate brightness among rock 'n' roll's brightest stars: 'Who's going to take the place of this band when it's gone?'

AC/DC ALBUM CHART HISTORY

	Chart placings for each album by country			Album certification by country		
	Aus	UK	US	Aus	UK	US
High Voltage (Aus.) 17 February 1975 Albert Productions	7	–	–			
T.N.T. (Aus.) December 1975 Albert Productions	2	–	–			
High Voltage 14 May 1976 Atlantic Records	–	–	146	–	Silver	3x Platinum
Dirty Deeds Done Dirt Cheap (Aus.) 20 September 1976 Albert Productions	4	–	–			

AC/DC ALBUM CHART HISTORY

	Chart placings for each album by country			Album certification by country		
	Aus	UK	US	Aus	UK	US
Dirty Deeds Done Dirt Cheap 17 December 1976 Atlantic Records	–	–	3	–	Silver	6x Platinum
Let There Be Rock (Aus.) 21 March 1977 Albert Productions	19	–	–			
Let There Be Rock 23 June 1977 Atlantic Records	–	17	154	–	Silver	2x Platinum
Powerage 25 May 1978 Atlantic Records	22	26	133	–	Silver	Platinum